SEARCH AT LOCH NESS

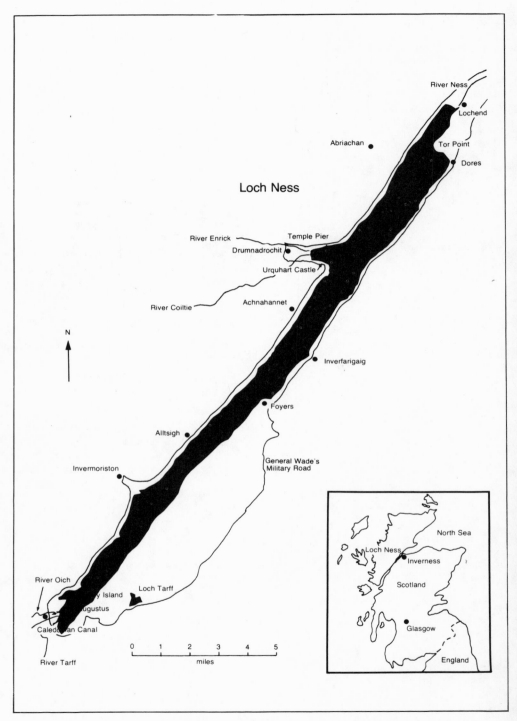

Loch Ness in northern Scotland (*Alumni Association of M.I.T.*)

SEARCH AT LOCH NESS

 The Expedition of
The New York Times and the
Academy of Applied Science

DENNIS L. MEREDITH

Quadrangle/The New York Times Book Co.

Designed by Beth Tondreau

Library of Congress Cataloging in Publication Data

Meredith, Dennis L
   Search at Loch Ness.

   Bibliography: p.
   1.   Loch Ness monster.   I.   New York times.
II.   Academy of Applied Science.   III.   Title.
QL89.2.L6M47   1977   001.9′44   76-50826
ISBN 0-8129-0677-2

To Joni

☙ Contents

SEARCH AT LOCH NESS

I do not know what I appear to the world, but to myself I seem to have been only like a boy playing on the sea-shore, and diverting myself in now and then finding a smoother pebble or a prettier shell than ordinary, whilst the great ocean of truth lay all undiscovered before me.

——Isaac Newton

I don't believe in that bullshit.

——Jacques Cousteau on the Loch Ness monster

🌰 Chapter One
THE VISITOR

It was June 19, 1975. The two yellow cylinders hanging in the murky waters rocked only slightly with the gentle flow of water. The cylinders were both lashed to the same long frame, one about five feet above the other. As they hung silently about 40 feet below the anchored, empty rowboat, the difference between them was apparent only briefly, every 75 seconds. Abruptly the top cylinder would emit a brilliant flash of light out into the waters, while the bottom cylinder clicked off a photograph of what the flash revealed.

For hundreds of flashes, the camera saw nothing but the swirling peat particles suspended in the brown water. This scarcity of photographic subjects was to be expected, for after all, relatively few creatures lived in the cold, barren waters of Loch Ness—it was not a hospitable environment.

At 9:45 P.M., as the late Scottish dusk settled on the loch, something approached the cylinders. A shape loomed out of the darkness, sweeping past in a swirl of water so quickly that the camera caught only a tantalizing, small slice of its surface in one film frame—a segment of flesh supporting—was it hairs? The camera waited, recording pictures as it had on countless occasions before in the loch. During this quiet period only an occasional eel or fish was caught by the strobe flash.

The camera was teased again an hour later, when the visitor returned from the darkness. Again the strobe was a fraction of a second too late, or perhaps too early, for all that was visible was a magnificent expanse of ugly yellow-mottled skin, with no features to indicate the visitor's nature. Perhaps these first encounters with the camera were merely the visitor's tentative reconnoitering of the strange apparatus. Perhaps the visitor quietly contemplated the strange mechanical device and decided upon a plan of aggression. Or perhaps the visitor merely thought of the camera as a possible dinner.

But whatever those first passes at the camera were, at 4:32 A.M., June 20, the photographic game between the camera and the visitor was escalated, with the camera winning the third round by capturing the visitor's image. The strobe light flashed with perfect timing, and froze onto the film a form that was a scientist's dream and a child's nightmare. Projecting up into the camera was a bulbous body, delicately curving into a slim, graceful neck which arched up the right side of the frame. For a short space on the frame, the image of the neck was obscured by shadow. Then there was a final splotch, suggestive of a head turned almost inquisitively toward the camera. Two appendages jutted out from the top of the body, and the effect was of a creature caught, surprised in the act of rushing the camera. But the next frame, 75 seconds later, showed nothing.

The camera was to pay for its intrusion; the cylinders almost immediately suffered a period of violent buffeting. So powerfully were they slammed by the unseen attacker that the 75-pound camera and strobe assembly was swung upward to photograph the bottom of the boat from which it hung.

There was a brief respite, and then around 5:40 A.M. the visitor again extracted revenge for the rude, brilliant flash it had suffered from the yellow cylinder. As the morning sun just rose over the loch, the camera shuddered again under the impact of a massive, invisible assailant. Again its frame was swung upward and again the camera photographed the underside of the boat. But the camera extracted a measure of revenge; it captured the image of a gnarled, gelatinous surface, so suffocatingly close to the camera that the surface almost obscured the lens. Again came blackness, and another six hours of monotonous flashing into the loch.

The sun had reached the zenith of its low arc across the Scottish sky when the ultimate confrontation between camera and visitor took place. The duel began as before with a series of bumps and bashes in which the camera was knocked upward to take photographs of the dim sun penetrating the brown waters, and then the boat and then the sun . . . and then, peering into the camera, its mouth open menacingly, a gargoyle. The dappled, grotesque head protruding into the film frame was the horned image of the legendary dragon, the fabled sea serpent. The peaty waters and the poor light obscured the face, transformed it into the hazy picture that the dreamer experiences as he desperately tries to clear his sleeping eyes to bring himself out of a nightmare. But it was there and it was shocking.

Then the nightmare melted into memory, left only on the film, as the hideous face disappeared. In the next frames only more violent buffeting was recorded. After a while, all was quiet again.

The camera continued to record little but peat particles until two hours later it was pulled from the water and into the boat. Its back was opened, its film was checked, and it was returned to the loch for what was to be its last encounter with the visitor—a final punctuation mark to the duel. At 4:50 P.M., two hours after the camera's examination, the visitor gave it a last sharp jounce, and the camera answered by capturing on film the silhouette of a rough surface against the dim sun.

To Robert Rines, the 16-mm. camera was an old familiar friend. It had originally come to him on loan from Harold E. "Doc" Edgerton, the renowned professor at the Massachusetts Institute of Technology who was the inventor of the strobe light. It was this camera that took earlier tantalizing pictures of a six-foot-long flipper deep under the loch on August 9, 1972. When Rines had released the strange photographs of a rhomboid-shaped flipper, they had excited monster-hunters everywhere, and skeptical scientists nowhere.

But on June 20, 1975, the 53-year-old Rines had no inkling of the incredible, violent encounters between his camera and the visitor, as he rowed out to retrieve the film. So, to him it was the same routine he had gone through countless times before—haul the camera out of the water, unscrew the bands holding the cover, withdraw the complex camera mechanism, and pull out the small metal film cassette.

And it was a routine flight back to the United States with the film tucked away in his luggage. All routine: leaving the film at the little Boston photo shop for developing—under bond to make sure there was no inadvertent tampering in processing—and finally picking the film up.

Rines, the lawyer-engineer, knew something about cameras and something about film, but he also knew that he would need more than average photographic expertise to prove his fervent belief that a huge unknown creature lived in Loch Ness. So, it was fortunate he had an old friend and a photographic genius rolled into one—Charlie Wyckoff.

It was late August 1975 when Rines finally had time to deliver the film to Charlie's small laboratory on the outskirts of Boston. Before going on to other business, they had taken a first quick look at the film—winding the film from one reel to another, over a light. Nothing. The pictures were so dark that the images remained obscured.

Still later, Charlie had wound the film past the light again. A dawning. On one frame was a mottled surface that Charlie took to be the bottom. But still the image had to take root and grow. Charlie Wyckoff, the analyst, did not yet understand that the first photograph he noticed could not have been the bottom; the camera had been over 30 feet above it. The mottled surface was only about ten feet away, and, in any case, the bottom was out of the camera's limited range in the dark loch. So there was no Eureka then; just a small-but-growing suspicion that something more than first met the eye had been captured on the roll of film taken beneath the loch.

On the morning of August 24, 1975, Charlie really began applying himself to the film. Sitting in his darkened office, the film projected on a screen, he began to click off the 2,000-picture roll, frame by frame. He knew from long experience never to be satisfied with a single look at anything; he would go back to worry the problem until it yielded all the information it possessed.

In the darkened room, Charlie put himself into the film; to really understand the film, he had to empathize with the camera. He almost *became* the camera eye itself seeing, click by click, what the camera had experienced. He sensed the motion of the camera from the subtle changes in light from frame to frame. He saw the swirling of particles in the deep loch, frame after frame. Then came the images, fascinating shapes isolated amidst hundreds of blank frames. It quickly dawned on Charlie that these objects were animate, that the pictures of the underside of the boat meant that something violent had happened to the camera during its period underwater. But still the meaning of the images eluded him. He knew only that they were important!

He wrote a careful, cool account of his early discoveries in his log:

"Every now and then a large object would appear in the frame," he wrote, "and shortly thereafter the camera gave the appearance of moving violently as evidenced by frames which record the water surface including a bottom view of the boat from which the camera was suspended. . . . These single frames of a large object were randomly distributed throughout the length of the film and are worthy of comment and further study."

Now he was certain that more was to be gleaned from the dark images on the film, so he went back to the beginning of the film to start over. He tightened his analytical grip, demanding more from each frame. He made careful notes on the appearance of each frame.

Of the first encounter Charlie wrote: "object lower left ¼ frame."

The second encounter: "Looks like picture of bottom, except it does not show light fall-off from one end to other. Object appears to be part of a large cylinder because of light fall-off top to bottom." (This meant that, while the top and bottom of the frame were in shadow, the left and right were not. The cone of light from a strobe would normally produce a circle of light on the bottom of the loch. Such a photograph of the circle of light would show the left, right, top, and bottom of the film frame in shadow.) "Object is a band ⅓ frame height running slight diagonal across frame," wrote Charlie. "This does not appear to be submerged log because of surface texture. It could be the skin of an animal."

The third encounter: "Mottled surface of object lower left frame has characteristic of animal with tube on head and long neck and side appendage. First appearance of boat in sequence. The next 20 frames show violent motion of camera as evidenced by boat at surface. This could have been caused by an object moving underwater near the camera causing turbulent water. Camera then quiets down during next 50 frames and then starts speeding up again."

Then came the strange picture of the gnarled surface, and then, much further on, the picture that would present the most intricate puzzle for Charlie—the horrible, nightmarish picture of the head.

Of it Charlie could then only write: "Object with exceedingly rough surface appears to cover all of left half of frame. Camera motion becoming very violent again for next 10 frames. Boat in view slightly enlarged as though camera nearer."

Charlie knew for certain now that these pictures were a complex symphony of light and shadow; he would have to experience them again and again to appreciate them. But he went on to the final shot. He wrote of the last blow in the underwater battle that had taken place months before, thousands of miles away:

"Rough textured surface body diagonally lower left half of frame."

By the time Charlie had completed his studies it was evening, and the images on the film had begun fitting together enough for Charlie to phone an excited Rines with the news.

Rines arrived at the lab the next day, and the two began poring over the film. The picture of the horrible head had them entranced. The two excitedly performed every analytical trick they could think of to get a better mental concept of the blurry images. They moved themselves to various places in the darkened room; they turned the slides of the pictures upside-down and sideways; they talked, they dreamed, they surmised. They knew that only a vigorous mixing of different approaches would yield the final true interpretation.

As they picked out the complex intertwinings of light and shadow, the picture of the head gradually sorted itself out in their minds. A hundred logical, small causes-and-effects on the picture began coalescing. A shadow on the face at one place meant a horn must have been sticking above the camera frame to cast the shadow; a bump, perhaps a nostril, on one side of the face corresponded with another bump on the other. There was a waltz of minds between Charlie and Rines, in which the jumble in the picture became a logical form. First Charlie recognized it: the picture was of a head peeking into the camera frame from the left side; its ugly mouth open toward the camera. But Rines needed more time; his mental set had to develop itself in its own way. He thought the picture of the head included an eye staring at him from the depths of the loch; Charlie interpreted the eye as a nostril with an open mouth beneath it. But most importantly, the object was a head and it was living! Nothing could wipe out that fact; no interpretation could escape from the fact that the image had been frozen onto the camera when the camera was being bashed around. And nothing could erase the fact that the image showed clear evidence of "bilateral symmetry"; a bump on one side was matched by a bump on the other," a horn on one side was matched by a horn on the other. Only living things and crystals show such natural symmetry. Rines and Wyckoff were able to transcend the poor quality of the picture, to use pure logic as their fuel, and it propelled them to the obvious conclusion that they had at last captured an underwater close-up of the fabulous Loch Ness monster!

Rines and Charlie were to continue their journey into the images all through September 1975. Charlie measured and sketched and calculated, noting his findings carefully in his log. Quietly figuring at his desk, he learned more and more about how things had been that day under the loch. He knew that the strobe's cone of light was angled a bit in relation to the camera's field of view. So the further away from the camera a large object was, the smaller the portion illuminated by the cone of light. *Voilà!* he had a way of measuring distances! Since, in the body-neck picture of the beast, the beam of light cut right across the creature's neck, his triangulation showed that the creature must have been 25 feet from the camera. To fill the film frame as it did, the portion of the creature in the film frame must have been about 20 feet long! And there was even more of the animal beyond the film frame!

There was another independent way of measuring the distance of that massive body from the camera. Light from the flash had been

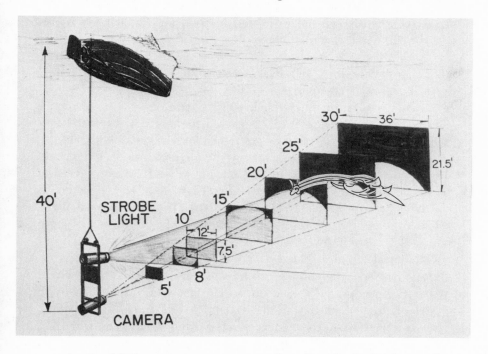

In the 1975 camera apparatus used under the loch, the strobe light beam and the camera's field of view were at an angle to one another, so the farther away the beast, the smaller the portion of the camera frame that was lighted. The light beam cut across the beast's neck, so the body must have been 25 feet away. (*Academy of Applied Science*)

robbed of its intensity in its journey through the peaty waters from the strobe to the creature and back to the camera. Charlie could use this as a yardstick by comparing the light density of the creature's image to the light from pictures of objects at known distances. From these calculations, again came out the magic number of 25 feet for the distance from creature to camera, and again Charlie calculated the portion of the creature in the frame to be about 20 feet.

Charlie had also figured out the size of the head, from the way the light struck it. The head had been so close to the camera that the beam from the strobe light had overshot it, transforming the head into a dark and ominous object in the frame. But the face was well in focus, and there was some stray light spilling onto it from the strobe beam. Thus, the head must have been out about five feet from the camera where it would be near, but not in, the light beam and where it would be in focus. Although the entire head was not in the camera frame, Charlie estimated that the whole thing was about two feet long, and the neck about 1½ feet thick. The open mouth, he calculated, was about six inches long and five inches wide. The creature's "horns" were about ten inches apart.

Slowly Charlie formed his final interpretation of the pictures, as he returned again and again for fresh examinations. He had learned over decades of photoanalysis to avoid mental traps—he withheld his judgments; let the evidence flow from the pictures into his mind; built his hypotheses of malleable mental images which he could remold or throw out as new evidence revealed itself to him. There would be plenty of time for hardened hypotheses later. Then they'd need Rines' skills as a lawyer—a brilliant, persuasive advocate for those hypotheses. Each in its own time.

On August 29, after going over the films thoroughly with Charlie, Rines had made a telephone call he was later to regret—to Nicholas Witchell, a young law student in Britain who had aided Rines in his past searches. Witchell was the author of *The Loch Ness Story*, a persuasive account of the evidence on the strange beast, and had asked to be allowed to chronicle Rines' expeditions. It was an excited Rines who blurted out to him on the transatlantic line, "Nick, we've got it; we've hit the jackpot. We have detailed close-up color photographs of the head, neck and body of one of the animals." Witchell immediately made plans to journey to America, to sit in on all the meetings and to witness the plans to release the pictures. The story of these new pictures would make an ideal ending for the paperback version of his book, due out that fall. But eager editors would soon spoil Witchell's triumph and Rines' along with it.

Rines also contacted George Zug, Curator of the Division of Reptiles and Amphibians of the Smithsonian Institution. Zug had encouraged Rines' research in the past, and would be delighted to examine the new pictures. In a September 2, 1975, meeting Rines, Wyckoff, Edgerton and Zug spent hours poring over the photographs. Zug was struck most by the head shot, and the evidence of bilateral symmetry. Launching into a bout of theorizing—by what Wyckoff had reported of his analysis—Zug speculated that photographs of the skin might show freshwater parasites; and that a dark area in one photograph might be the animal's anal fold. He was to be embarrassed later when his off-the-cuff ideas were indelibly recorded in Witchell's book. But Zug was firmly convinced that Rines had captured the image of a huge animal with his underwater camera.

News of Rines' photographs had spread rapidly to the *National Geographic*, which prompted a letter to Rines from the editors—raising the prospect of large sums of money for the photographs. It was on September 6 that the editors journeyed to Wyckoff's laboratory to view the photographs. In the darkroom, the *Geographic* editors were spellbound at the sight of the pictures.

"Jesus Christ, look at that!" exclaimed Gilbert Grosvenor, editor of the magazine, according to Witchell. Witchell faithfully recorded the exclamation, not realizing that the editors would repudiate what was said, once they realized what they would face in advocating the existence of the fabled beast. But at the meeting the enthusiastic editors said they would definitely publish the photographs in the January, 1976, issue of the magazine, which would appear December 8 or 9, 1975. A timetable was set; Rines would begin arranging a scientific meeting to present the pictures on December 9; following this would be a meeting at the House of Commons in London at which Parliament would be presented with the evidence. Parliament was considering legislation to protect the beast in the loch, and the new evidence would be an excellent way to persuade them that the creature existed and that protection was needed. It was all a grand and glorious scheme. Rines set off to make the plans.

But Rines had not counted on a peculiar phenomenon he was later to experience time and time again when he showed people the pictures. As each group would see the photographs that winter, there would be at first awe, then excitement. In the darkened room the pictures of the head would inspire a rapturous bout of theorizing, dreaming, planning. Careful questions were easily forgotten in the world of monsters; careful answers were easily missed. But in the cold light outside Charlie's office, or perhaps on the flight home, or even sitting at one's desk the next day with a familiar coffee cup in one's hand, things would change for those who had seen the pictures. Doubts would well up.

"After all, these are pretty poor pictures. . . ."

"After all, who are these monster-hunters anyway?"

"After all, this is *the Loch Ness monster* they claim to have photographed!"

"After all, this may not be good for one's reputation. . . ."

Those who had seen the pictures would fight an internal battle between pure logic—the analysis of the pictures—and the infection of that logic by all the history of doubts, hoaxes, and emotion surrounding the beast. As had happened so many times before, the fabulous nature of the beast would once more lead to a denial of its existence by otherwise sensible people confronted with otherwise sensible data.

At the *Geographic* the "after all's" mounted.

Joseph Judge, one of the editors was later to remember his impression in a magazine interview:

"I'm not saying that the material is a fake, but the picture of the head and neck looked just what a monster of the deep should look like. The gaping mouth, that long bony ridge running down the center of its face, the oval eyes with frilly ridges around them . . . like Puff the Magic Dragon."

A month later, after Rines had settled arrangements for the scientific symposium, the *Geographic* had an attack of qualms, and Rines was left to seek another outlet for the photographs. Rines, Wyckoff, and Rines' brother-in-law, Robert Needleman, approached *Time* magazine. Again the viewers at *Time* were captivated by the magic of the pictures, again they were stricken with the virus of doubt, and again they became timid, wary of somehow being made the suckers. Like the *Geographic* editors, those at *Time* edged cagily out of the picture, but in *Time*'s case the negotiations ended sourly when an exasperated Rines called and demanded his pictures back. The bad feelings would show up later in a cynical *Time* article lampooning Rines and his pictures.

Over the next month, rumors of amazing pictures began to spread in Britain. Printers preparing the paperback edition of Witchell's book, which contained the description of the photographs, began placing bets on the monster's existence. Word began to leak out on the scientific symposium, which had been scheduled at the University of Edinburgh, sponsored by the university and the Royal Society of Scotland. Perhaps the rumors would have remained but ripples on the public consciousness, and the scientific society would have had first crack at judging the photographs. Rines had avoided the press and his dam of silence was holding, even though many newspapers had set their reporters after him to learn the secrets of the photographs. Unfortunately for Rines, one newspaper editor at the Glasgow *Sunday Mail* came into possession of information that was too good to keep secret—the galleys of Witchell's book—and on November 23, 1975, he splashed Witchell's description of the beast all over the newspaper's front page. "The head was ugly. Gargoyle was the word that came to mind!" screamed the headline quoting Witchell. "It was hideous, angular, bony and revolting!" Then came another blow: the repudiation of the photographs by scientists at the British Museum of Natural History, who were among the experts Rines had asked to examine the photographs.

The zoologists were of five minds on what the photographs showed, and on the existence of the legendary beast itself, but they spoke as one, united against the onslaught of the press and of the photographs. The scientists were Gordon Sheals, Keeper of Zoology; G. B. Corbet, Deputy Keeper of Zoology; Humphrey Greenwood, of the Department of Zoology's Fish Section; H. W. Ball, Keeper of Paleontology; and Alan Charig, Curator of Fossil Reptiles. They were nicknamed the "Kensington Five" by the press—the museum is located in the South Kensington section of London—and they had been chosen by the press, the public, and the betting parlors as the final arbiters of the Loch Ness evidence.

"None of the photographs is sufficiently informative to establish the existence, far less the identity of a large animal in the loch," the five sniffed in unison in a November 24, 1975 news release. But their next sentence, concerning Rines' 1972 pictures of the large flipper taken under Loch Ness, revealed that they were actually puzzled over Rines' photographs.

"With regard to the photographs taken in 1972, Dr. Zug of the United States National Museum of Natural History, had said that 'computer enhancement of one frame produces a flipperlike object.' [We] cannot disagree with this comment, but the information in this photograph is insufficient to enable [us] to attempt even the broadest identification."

The clever use of a double negative—"cannot disagree"—helped them to back nervously away from the fact that the Kensington Five concurred that the 1972 photo showed a flipper. And the plea of "insufficient information" seemed to be a scientists' copout. It must have been embarrassing to the experts, when confronted with the clear outline of a flipper, taken in the depths of Loch Ness, to admit that they couldn't figure it out. Even with their extensive combined past experiences at examining all manner of animal tails, flippers, fins, and legs, they could not fit this one on any known creature, and certainly couldn't link it with any creature common to the loch. The zoologists seemed desperately to want to be able to assign Rines' pictures to some safe, familiar animal, for they performed veritable intellectual handsprings in attempts to explain away the 1975 pictures. Of the picture of the animal's body and neck:

"We are intrigued by the reflectivity of this object. It occurred to some of us that this might be attributable to the presence of a large number of small gas bubbles such as are found in the air sacs of the larvae of phantom midges which are known to occur in large swarms. . . . These insects are known to occur in Scottish lochs but we have no data on their abundance nor on the size of their swarms." It was a peculiar, eccentric speculation, almost as remarkable as the idea of a Loch Ness monster. The scientists were proposing that a mass of tiny insects, on which they had no information, formed themselves into precisely this shape, swept in front of the camera, and vanished, never to be seen again. Perhaps it seemed easier at the time than admitting to a monster.

The picture of the head also afforded a chance for pirouettes of logic:

"To one of us it strongly suggested the head of a horse with bridle," wrote the museum scientists, "and others conceded this likeness when it was pointed out. The size limits are compatible with this explanation. On this interpretation, eyes, ears, noseband, and nostrils are visible, along with a less clear structure that could represent a neck.

"We believe that the image is too imprecise for us to argue that this does indeed represent a dead horse, but we equally believe that such an interpretation cannot be eliminated." The description of the head as resembling a horse was unintentionally ironic; the Loch Ness monster had long been linked with the legendary "water-horse," a creature of Scottish legend.

Everybody was getting into the game of denouncing the pictures. At a news conference, Sir Frank Claringbull, director of the museum, could not resist his own snipe: "It's a piece of tree."

With this official damnation and the subsequent cancellation of the Edinburgh conference (too much publicity spoils the science, contended the timid sponsors) the photographs became the target of every "expert" in Britain, and the newspapers dutifully gave each one headlines.

The 1975 photographs were transformed by press stories into a lost Viking ship, a diver with his mask on backward, or a fake movie monster lost in the loch, depending on which newspaper one read.

Throughout the storm, Rines held on, keeping to himself and waiting for his chance to redeem his photographs—the December 10, 1975, meeting in the British House of Commons. He refused to talk to the press, believing his time would come; and the press took his silence to mean one of two things: either Rines was a fraud or he had the most remarkable pictures in history. Either way it was one hell of a story, and they meant to get it.

So when Rines, his wife, his baby son, and his mother-in-law arrived in London's Heathrow Airport for the December 10 House of Commons meeting, they were besieged by reporters. Waves of reporters met Rines at the airport, followed him to his hotel, and camped in the lobby waiting for some word.

Safe in the quiet of his room, Rines and his family looked forward to a little respite before the meetings to follow. Then came a knock on the door, and the nasal British inquiry that Rines was to hear time and again in his nightmares. "Duktuh Roines? A few questions, please?"

Hour after hour, reporters knocked at his door, slipped notes under it, and phoned him. Rines and his wife Carol became worried. A considerable amount of money had been bet on the validity of these pictures, and their irrefutable proof of the beast's existence. Was there the possibility of some kidnap attempt, or a mob scene? Who knew? Rines resolved to remove himself and his family from the watchful eyes of the press.

With the help of Charlie Wyckoff and Doc Edgerton's secretary, Jean Mooney, Rines' bags were sneaked out of the hotel past the unsuspecting reporters. Then followed Rines and his wife, seemingly on an innocent outing with their baby son. Then it was into a cab on to a secretly arranged hotel. Finally, peace at last!

But it was not to last long. On the evening of December 10, 1975, came the first public presentation of the photographs.

🌾 Chapter Two

THE MEETING

The formal unveiling of the new evidence was to take place in a three-hour symposium in a committee room in the House of Commons, Palace of Westminster. The meeting was arranged by David James, a member of Parliament, war hero, and long-time supporter of investigations at the loch. The huge room, ringed by tall windows hung with rich curtains, was packed, and even the standing room around the edge was occupied.

It was a gala event, not only for Rines and his cohorts, but for all the people who had taken up the banner of the Loch Ness monster. The monster-hunters, both current and past, would have the best chance ever to present their case in an imposing setting, and with scores of reporters and establishment scientists looking on. They would bring up their biggest guns.

The opening salvo was fired by Sir Peter Scott, the British naturalist who had captured Britain's attention a few years earlier with his announcement of belief in the Loch Ness monster. Sir Peter was a prominent fixture in Britain; the son of the famous Antarctic explorer Robert Falcon Scott, he had long championed the popular British cause of conservation through the World Wildlife Fund. Sir Peter's first duty in the House of Commons meeting was to explain the bestowal by him and Rines of a scientific name on the monster—*Nessiteras rhombopteryx*. The name was meant to give a scientific handle to the animal, on which to base laws to protect it. *Nessiteras* is a combination of the name of the loch, with the Greek word "teras" which means "wonder." *Rhombopteryx* is a combination of the Greek "rhombos" for "diamond or lozenge shape" and the Greek "pteryx" meaning "fin" or "wing." Thus, the mysterious beast that had inhabited the loch for thousands of years entered the scientific world as "Ness-wonder with the diamond-shaped fin." With the publication of an article by Scott and Rines the next day in the British journal *Nature*, the world would know of the new scientific name.

Quietly, conservatively, Scott recited to the audience the logic that had led him to champion the cause of the monster.

"Now when you see the pictures and hear the evidence, you may think as I do that there are three possible explanations. The first is that the people who obtained this evidence are perpetrating a hoax or deception. The second is that they are the victims of a hoax perpetrated by a third party. And, the third one is that the pictures are genuine.

"I have considered these possibilities very carefully, and I am entirely satisfied that the first does not apply. Nor do I think it possible—and I think you will agree when you see the evidence—that they have been hoaxed. And this leads me to the only acceptable hypothesis, which is the third—that the pictures are genuine and they are representations of animal structures."

With this, Sir Peter introduced Rines, and the press got their first good look at the man who for two months had played a game of cat-and-mouse with them.

Rines stood easily in front of the audience, a man of medium height, blond and in his 50s. The audience saw the son of a brilliant patent lawyer, himself a brilliant patent lawyer. They saw a headstrong, independent man who expected the same fierce independence of thought in others that he expected of himself. He had begun college at M.I.T. in the late 1930s, but puzzled his father by wanting to part company with the Institute to write opera. But during World War II, he had become interested in radar, and he returned to M.I.T. from the army and graduated in 1942, by then credited with several inventions in radar and sonar. Toward the end of the war he had studied law at Georgetown University in Washington, D.C., obtaining a J.D. degree, and he later earned a Ph.D. at National Chiao Tung University in Taiwan.

Two themes have dominated Rines' professional and intellectual life. First, is his belief that technology has not been given its due;

that there is too little recognition of its place in society. Second is his conviction that too little help and encouragement has been given the independent inventor and entrepreneur in a government-dominated America. Rines, the patent lawyer, had aided many inventors to secure the rewards of their ingenuity, but he wanted to do more. In 1963 Rines and a group of friends founded a private organization called the Academy of Applied Science to act as an umbrella for their projects in aiding technology and inventors.

Rines' advocacy of the entrepreneur took other forms. He believed that able lawyers were needed to wrest the rightful fruits of an inventor's ingenuity from government bureaucrats. So Rines helped found the Franklin Pierce Law Center in New Hampshire, a law school dedicated to turning out such lawyers.

The search for the beast in the loch fitted well the themes of Rines' life. His expeditions drew on new techniques of underwater photography, sonar, and chemistry, demonstrating the power of technology. And he would lead his fellow technologists into a realm of research shunned by official zoology, proving the need for individual initiative in a world of stodgy, institutionalized science.

As a lawyer, Rines was confident of his power to persuade, to grab an audience with his words, carry them through his argument, and set them down at the conclusion he wished. It was as if he possessed a switch that could click over from the cool, introverted, private Rines to the hot, persuasive, public Rines. His lawyer-switch was turned on for this occasion.

Rines began his speech in Parliament grandly, his flat Boston accent certainly sounding strange to British ears:

"Lord Chairman, Lords, Members of Parliament, members of the scientific community, members of the press, distinguished visitors.

"This is indeed an honor, particularly as an American, to be able to address you in these revered halls and particularly as we in America approach our 200th birthday to reflect that we did, indeed, get many of our ideas about freedom and freedom of speech from your ancestors here in Great Britain." As Rines warmed to his subject, a touch of gospel preacher was added to the lawyer's powerful cadences. He used pauses, inflection, and intonation masterfully to carry the audience with him.

"I feel very gratified that we have an opportunity to present the truth as we have found it and, indeed, to let the scientific community the world over judge whether, as we think we have done, we have opened a crack that may lead to 'official' scientists' no longer being afraid to come to Loch Ness and explore, not just the matter of large animals, but the *tremendously interesting limnological and geological wonder that you have in the British Isles and Scotland!*"

Rines the showman gave the audience a teasing preview of what was to come, as he flashed onto the large screen, the 1972 flipper picture. The grainy black-and-white slide floated tantalizingly in front of the audience, challenging them to identify it. With a lawyer's flair for drama, he then sprung on the audience a picture that few had seen before: another flipper picture taken only seconds before the first. The slightly different shape and positioning of the flipper in the second picture revealed that it was animate; that it had moved! The images lingered in the mind; the audience suddenly empathized, identified with the camera, as it had sat on the bottom of the loch watching the powerful six-foot flipper weaving through the water.

"Now, if you would come with me up to northern Scotland to Loch Ness, which is a tremendous natural wonder," continued Rines, "everybody thinks that the local chamber of commerce creates its monster each year. But if you really look at the terrain and see the precipitous mountains that come down and form the boundaries of this deep gorge some 750 feet deep in places—a gorge that extends 25 miles or so diagonally from Inverness across a good portion of northern Scotland—you will see that there are no tourist traps."

He flashed a map of the long narrow loch onto the screen.

"Loch Ness extends from the Ness River—which empties into the Moray Firth of the North Sea—and is the first of a string of lochs which proceed diagonally across Scotland to the Irish Sea.

"It is the biggest of those lochs, and about one-third of the way down the loch is a bay where we did most of our operations— Urquhart Bay—and this bay is fed by rivers—the Enrick and Coiltie. At times the rivers are bone dry. Salmon and sea trout of different types come up from the North Sea at different times of the year, jump into Loch Ness which is 50 feet above sea level, and come into the bay and go into these rivers, as well as other rivers, to spawn.

"Part of the technology we used was to wait for that time when the salmon were, indeed, up to spawn and when the rivers were sufficiently dry that they couldn't get up there and, therefore, we had a teeming fish population in the bay." Rines had carried his audience to the loch. Now he would introduce them to the man who had been indirectly responsible for the entire project, the famous "Doc" Edgerton.

Doc calmly ambled forward and began his offhand speech on taking underwater pictures with strobe lights. He is a man of 72, who looks 52, has the razor-sharp mind of a 32-year-old, and the unending, delightful inquisitiveness of a two-year-old. He talks in an easy shorthand, skipping phrases, jumbling words, but carrying the listener along with the logic of what you know he meant to say.

Doc's formal credentials seem not to fit with the relaxed, easy-going scientist. He is an Institute Professor Emeritus at M.I.T., a title reserved for only the most eminent scientists there. His honors stretch on and on: the U.S. National Medal of Science, the Royal Society of London's Silver Medal, the Richardson Medal of the Optical Society of America, the John Oliver LaGorce Gold Medal of the National Geographic Society, membership in the National Academy of Science and the National Academy of Engineering. . . .

But the heavy load of honors results precisely from Doc's steady, easy personality. He is not the scientist who flashes into brilliance with a leap of scientific intuition, only to fade. Rather, he is like the invention he perfected in the 1930s: the strobe light. Periodically, effortlessly, he dazzles with some feat of brilliance. He is called "Papa Flash" by the admiring crew of the explorer Jacques Cousteau's ship *Calypso*, whom he introduced to underwater photography.

Papa Flash has orchestrated some of the most incredible high-speed photographs ever taken. During World War II, he flew over France in a bomber fitted with a huge strobe and flooded miles of terrain with instantaneous flashes of light, taking photographs to be used in planning troop movements. His flash strobes and cameras have caught bullets in mid-flight, frozen a hummingbird's wings, and stilled a drop of milk as it splashed into a still pool, creating a delicate crown of droplets.

Doc is a man with the heart of a teacher, a mind like a bear trap, and the soul of a con artist. He is also a clever instigator of others, deriving enormous enjoyment from watching people he has taught tackling tough problems. His cluttered laboratory at M.I.T. has spewed forth eager, motivated young scientists like embers from a Fourth-of-July sparkler. He instigated Rines' Loch Ness expeditions the same way he has done countless other projects. He curtly informs the proposers of projects that their ideas couldn't possibly work, gives them the tools to try, and watches, a twinkle in his eye, as they speed off to prove him wrong.

Doc first met Rines when Rines was 11, brought to an Edgerton lecture by his father David Rines, who was Doc's patent lawyer. After that lecture, Edgerton recalled, the young Rines rushed up front brimming with questions, he was so excited. Edgerton knew how to handle Rines when he approached Doc 40 years later with a proposal that they look for the Loch Ness monster. He told the audience in Parliament:

"Rines came in one day, and he said, 'I want you to help take pictures of the monster in Loch Ness.' And I said, 'Nothing doing; I don't want to have anything to do with anything like that because I'm a serious scientist. But I will loan you equipment if you will take a picture of what is in that lake, because there's nothing like experimentation in this world. You must go out in the field and get data on what is there.'

"A person must never be intimidated or influenced in any way, shape or form by anybody; he must go and get data, and electronic flash is a way to do it."

With this story, Doc demonstrated to the audience the strobe and camera cylinders that he had developed to take underwater pictures, and which had been loaned to Rines for his expeditions. He flicked the switch on the camera. "It's really quite simple equipment."

Suddenly a blinding flash lit up the audience, an unseemly shock of light which jarred them out of their complacency. Doc had taken their picture. "This is not a very bright unit," said Doc modestly, enjoying his little photographic attack, as he made for his chair.

Rines had led expeditions to the loch every year since 1970. In 1972 and 1975 he had obtained the hazy underwater pictures with Doc's gear, but in 1970 luck had given him his first evidence for the creature —sonar contacts with a large moving underwater object. Sonar expert Martin Klein had operated the sonar in 1970, and it was the blips from Klein's machine that put a gut-wrenching reality into the monster for Rines. Before, the beast had been merely an intellectual exercise, a creature existing only in past photographs, old sonar charts, and vague eyewitness reports. Rines next introduced Klein to the audience in Parliament and he told them what he had seen on the 1970 trip to the loch.

"It was an enormous privilege and challenge when Bob Rines asked if I'd be interested in going to Loch Ness to use our sonars to look for the monster," said Klein.

"Our machines had already been used all over the world to find ancient shipwrecks, to study the geology of the sea bottom, and in other industrial applications. . . . But in Loch Ness we really had a different challenge, and that challenge was to use our sonar, which is normally towed through the water, to find a large moving object.

"Our idea was to take the sonar and mount it in a stationary position, so that if a moving object went by it, there would be absolutely no question that the object would be moving," said Klein.

Klein was proud of the power of his stationary sonar idea. The beam of sound pulsing into the water could not only penetrate the murky waters of the loch, but also rule out automatically rocks, logs, pilings, and the other stationary objects, allowing clear-cut information on what moved beneath the surface. Klein showed the audience how the presence of a stationary object in the sonar beam would leave a continuous straight-line trace as the paper sonar chart reeled out of the recorder. The object would be always there, always echoing the probing sonar beam from the same place, the same way.

However, a moving object would show up on the chart as a suddenly appearing, diagonal trace on the paper, cutting through the straight-line traces of stationary objects. And this is what happened on Rines' expeditions in 1970 and later in 1972. Klein showed the trace obtained one day in 1970, a large chart with small dark splotches where objects had appeared in the beam far out in the loch.

"From my other work in the loch and my work in many bodies of water around the world," said Klein, "I determined that whatever was going by here [in 1970] was very much larger than the little fish that had been passing the sonar earlier in our work; in fact, I would estimate that whatever we're seeing here was somewhere in the neighborhood of 10 to 50 times as big as the other fish we had seen.

"Now, the other exciting thing about the target was the fact that it is solid. I've had lots of experience using the sonar to look at things like schools of fish and gas bubbles . . . they do not look solid. However, this echo did look solid . . . this was very exciting, so we kept on monitoring. . . . And we were heartened to find that about half an hour later, and then again another 15 minutes later, we picked up similar targets out at a distance. . . . To me, this indicated we really had a moving object, we didn't simply have a log that was slowly drifting. We did have a moving object that was coming in and out of the sonar beam."

Klein understood that his sonar machine was unfamiliar to laymen and scientists alike, and that they would mistrust this new way of seeing with sound. So, besides making a profession of manufacturing and selling sonar machines, he had made a hobby of using them to find objects on the ocean floor. He wanted to *prove* over and over that what sonar said lay on the bottom was actually there, whether it be a ship, a pipeline, or a rock outcropping.

Klein's personality matched sonar well. He was unequivocal, straightforward, analytical. He did not advocate, but reported, in a calm, deep voice, emanating from behind a glorious walrus mustache. He was another of the sparks from Doc's laboratory. He had received his degree from M.I.T. and had immediately gone to work as an engineer for EG&G, the electronics company Doc had helped found. Klein had been a chief engineer in charge of developing the first commercial "side-scan" sonar machines, so named because they blanket the ocean bottom with beams of sound from the sides of a torpedo-shaped "fish" towed behind a boat. The fish sends out a thin vertical fan of pulses, using transducers in its sides, which both produce the pulses and receive the echoes. The return signals are played out on a recorder on board the boat, which prints them out as patterns of dark tracings showing what the reflected sound waves have seen. At EG&G Klein had discovered where improvements could be made in the EG&G sonar, and had founded his own small company to build better sonar devices.

The audience examined Klein's sonar tracings on the screen. The black splotches of sonar were simultaneously more authoritative to the scientists, and more mistrusted by them. A sonar scan was more authoritative because few could dispute the sheer, powerful logic that a beam of sound coursing out from a sonar transducer could echo only from something solid in its path. There could be no arguing with a nice solid sonar echo. Critics might carp that the reflection could be from something falsely solid, like bubbles from a boat wake. Such an objection was easily answered by making sure that there were no boats in the area when sonar was operating. A little care and the logic of sonar was irresistible.

Sonar was also more mistrusted. It was an alien way of seeing, not like the familiar sense of sight, which depends on light bouncing off an object. Underwater photographs at least gave the zoologists an out. Photographs could be more readily disputed as tricks of light or faked negatives. This nasty business of sonar logic disturbed the scientists. And so the zoologists confronted with sonar evidence for the beast simply muttered and went about their business.

Klein's 1970 sonar contact had been exciting, but it was after the 1972 incident, when Rines used a combination of sonar and cameras, that the world began to be convinced that Rines was onto something. Rines now stood to become the storyteller for the audience in the House of Commons symposium, telling his tale as if to wide-eyed campers around a too-small fire in a dark forest.

The 1972 pictures were obtained on the night of August 8, said Rines, a rare evening when the loch was flat and calm. Rines and friends from the British Loch Ness Investigation Bureau had anchored their boats a short distance offshore. They lowered a sonar transducer into the water and gently settled it onto a sloping underwater ridge, aiming its beam out into the dark loch. From another boat, was lowered the Edgerton camera, settled farther down the slope. The camera and strobe cylinders were strapped together on a metal stand, flashing away periodically at the area where the sonar beam was aimed. The investigators waited throughout the beautiful Scottish night, watching the paper unfurl slowly from the sonar recorder on the boat.

"And then, about 1:40 in the morning the team aboard the sonar boat was startled—the hair went up on the backs of their necks—to see coming in here this same solid type of trace that we hit in 1970," said Rines.

The dark smear coming out on the paper had burned itself into their minds. Something was there! Something large. Just a few dozen yards from the boat—unseen—was the animal they had sought!

The dark trace on the sonar chart disappeared as rapidly as it had come. The animal had gone, and the men could only hope that it had come close enough to the clicking camera for pictures of whatever it was. The tension drained away and the team contemplated the probability of another long wait.

But suddenly, minutes later, salmon began splashing to the surface of the loch, desperately trying to escape something beneath. The salmon showed on the sonar as thread-like lines across the paper. Abruptly the dark trace reappeared stronger than before. The beast had returned! Unknown to the men, their underwater camera then first captured the pictures of flippers, as the beast hovered in front of the lens. After a few heart-stopping minutes, the beast was gone for good, and Rines was left on the gently rocking boat to savor what had happened.

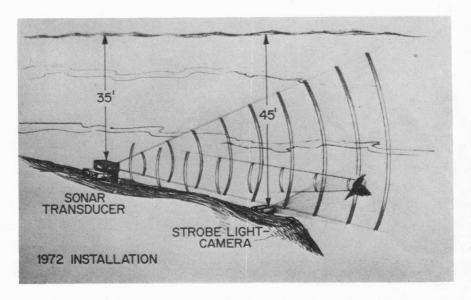

The 1972 camera and sonar apparatus that captured the flipper pictures. (*Academy of Applied Science*)

Excitedly he had the color films developed, he told the audience in Parliament, only to discover that the loch had defeated him. The floating peat particles and the suspended muck had reflected the powerful strobe light back into the camera. Rines flashed onto the screen in the committee room the photographs, which were obscured by an ugly, brown fog.

But Rines was not licked yet, he told the audience. On two photographs he could discern a vague shape, and these photographs had been taken at the same time the sonar said there was a large moving object near the camera. Rines sent those vague pictures to his friend Alan Gillespie at the Jet Propulsion Laboratories of the California Institute of Technology. Scientists there had developed a remarkable "computer enhancement" process whereby a computer could scan photographs, discern where light intensity on the photograph changed abruptly from the background, and enhance the contrast between those areas and the background. The process had been used extensively in space research to transform the fuzzy pictures of planets taken from space probes into clear pictures of other worlds. And forensic scientists had used computer enhancement to clear up pictures of smudged fingerprint patterns, revealing identifiable patterns of loops and whorls.

In the case of Rines' 1972 flipper pictures, the computer had done wonders. The computer-enhanced slides he showed the audience in Parliament were clearly pictures of an animal flipper. But still the zoologists in the audience were suspicious, as they had been when the evidence was first released in 1972. They were unfamiliar with what the computer had done to the pictures, and with unfamiliarity came distrust. The zoologists seemed to focus on the computer enhancement as symptomatic of their distrust of all the technology Rines had bombarded them with: the sonar, the underwater cameras, the strobe lights —all were odd pieces of equipment far removed from the tweezers, microscopes, and other familiar objects to the zoologists.

The results of Rines' technology had surprised even him. Submitting his 1972 sonar records to a number of experts, he had received the unexpected news that during one period there had been *two* animals in his sonar beam that night, not just one! So, as a long shot, Rines had handed over to Gillespie the film frames taken by the underwater camera during that period. Amazingly, one frame showed two large blobs hovering in the distance, the film grains barely spelling out what could be interpreted as a massive body with flipper hanging down, and another body just protruding into the film. Measuring the images, the photographic scientists had determined that the objects were about 12 feet apart, just as the sonar experts had said.

Rines presented these discoveries to the audience in Parliament with evident pride in the abilities of his technologies, but some of the zoologists were certainly uncomfortable with this further example of magic. Rines was merciless, hammering home his conclusion from the 1972 pictures; a touch of hellfire and brimstone in his voice.

"And so, we show you here this checking on each other of sonar that unambiguously discriminates against stationary objects as Marty Klein told you—and positively tells you they're moving objects," said Rines.

"And here we're talking about those unenhanced [1972 flipper] pictures that we couldn't make much of, and the computer clearing away the silt showed us these two giant appendages and showed us two animal structures here. . . ."

Rines brought on further ammunition, introducing a statement by Alan Gillespie on the powers and legitimacy of computer enhancement:

"It is not possible to insert patterns resembling monsters or anything else using these independent processes," said Gillespie's statement. "Filter artifacts will not introduce objects resembling monsters or anything else into pictures which do not contain them. Filtering will, however, exaggerate local contrast and is thus very useful, because contrast changes and poorly illuminated regions can be optimally displayed in the same picture as contrast changes in well-lit regions."

Doc Edgerton then gave the audience his simple reasoning for concluding that the flipper was huge and far away from the camera, and not merely a minnow fin close-up:

"We are certain that the in-focus diagonal object [the flipper] that you see running across the frame is approximately six feet long," said Doc. "If this object were shorter than six feet, it would need to be closer to the camera [to fill the frame] and would therefore be out of focus, as is, indeed, the portion of the picture on the right-hand side."

After seeing the 1972 pictures, Charlie Wyckoff was persuaded to join Rines in the search, and they had developed the camera systems to be used over the next three years. Rines and Wyckoff rose to tell the audience in Parliament the story of their next success at the loch, in 1975. Charlie had improved Rines' photographic setup immensely, he explained, by the simple ploy of separating the camera and strobe light on the supporting frame. With the camera right next to the strobe light, the flashes had bounded off the cloud of peat particles in the water right back into the camera lens—like the light from auto headlamps in a fog bouncing back at the driver, spoiling his vision. But with the camera and light separated, the interfering light would tend to reflect away from the camera.

In 1975, Rines and Wyckoff told the audience, there had been triumph, but also failure. Near the flashing 16-mm. Edgerton camera, hung from a boat, had been another camera system resting on the bottom that Rines had really pinned his hopes on. Mounted on a tall frame well clear of the bottom was a sophisticated camera-strobe unit attached to a sonar transducer beaming outward at the camera's field of view. The camera would wait passively, conserving its film until a computer attached to the sonar and reading the results from the sonar beam decided that a large object had intruded in front of the camera. Only then would the computer trigger the camera to begin flashing off pictures. It was a lovely system, and in the weeks it had been on the bottom, it had been triggered by large underwater objects several times, taking 96 pictures . . . of mud. When the beast had first swam in front of the camera, thought Rines and Wyckoff, it had stirred up the fine brown silt, which had covered the camera lens. Once more the loch had protected its secret.

But still there was the Edgerton camera, now dubbed "Old Faithful." It continued to flash away, obtaining the 1975 pictures. As Rines triumphantly projected those remarkable pictures on the screen in Parliament he lingered dramatically over each one, inviting the zoologists in the audience to analyze, to speculate . . . for God's sake, *to dream!*

"We prefer to leave it to the zoologists and scientists to study this and other material that we have produced, some of which is in more dispute. . . . Whether they say it's an animal or not an animal, they can't deny that it's any unexplained phenomenon!" he exclaimed.

But all the drama in the world wouldn't save unconvincing evidence, and it was Charlie Wyckoff who added sound logical backup to Rines' conviction that the photographs showed the monster. In the next segment of the symposium, Charlie presented his reasoning on the 1975 photographs. Charlie was a showman in his own way, flashing on the screen slides which compared the picture of the huge body with that of a small eel, and showing slides explaining how the light cone cutting across the frame convinced him the animal was 25 feet from the camera. Charlie disdained the usual slides scientists show in their lectures, with mounds of confusing numbers arranged in complex charts and tables. Charlie was a photographer who knew how to use images to make his point.

Charlie Wyckoff, as always, was calm, optimistic, steady. He explained his work clearly, but with little of the drama used by Rines. He was a professional scientist, and he had learned over the years that enthusiasm must be conserved and parceled out carefully. There always had to be a reserve to get through the boredom or frustration that often afflicts science. His easy reserve had

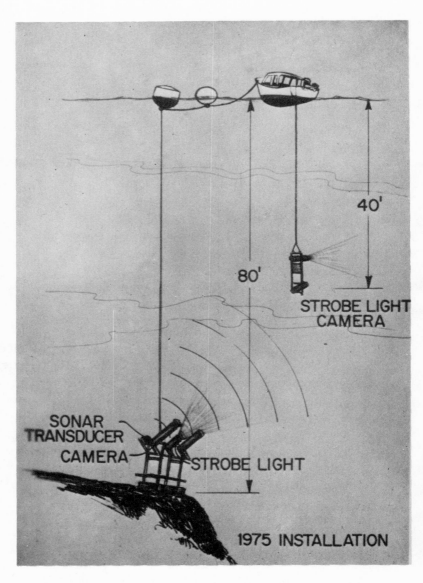

The 1975 camera apparatus featured a sonar-activated camera on the bottom, and Old Faithful, flashing away, hanging nearby. (*Academy of Applied Science*)

kept him young. With a full head of dark hair, a spare, short frame, and hazel eyes, he looked younger than a man of 59.

Charlie, another of Doc Edgerton's pupils at M.I.T., had dedicated his life to capturing on film images new to human experience. He used cameras to freeze those incredible moments too fleeting, too blinding, or too subtle for unaided man to experience. Immediately after college, working for EG&G, he had developed methods to capture on film the violence of underwater explosions. In the seesaw of invent-and-destroy so typical of military research, he had helped the navy develop better underwater mines and torpedos, and then better ships to withstand them, and then better explosions to blow up those ships, and then better ships, and so on.

After World War II, he transferred his talents to photographing the brilliant flashes of nuclear explosions. He became the impresario of huge arrays of cameras arrayed around blast sites and ingeniously triggered to capture the first moments of the explosions. Charlie's cameras performed exquisitely to capture the awesome destructive images which astounded and frightened a world thrust into the atomic age.

Charlie is a modest man. When he talks of his inventions, he says they were "conjured"—as if they appeared in his mind through some process other than his own ingenuity. Thus, when NASA needed a special film for its moon landing program, Charlie "conjured" it. The giant film companies said that nobody could invent a single film to record simultaneously the bright surface of a sunlit moon and the fathomless darkness of its shadows. Charlie's simple act of conjuring proved them dead wrong, and the astronauts took Charlie's film to the moon with them. From the film used on the moon he has since conjured a "hi-fi" color film which makes usual color film look pale and lifeless. His remarkable experimental color film records the depth and delicacy of color that only the human eye could see before. But it is only a simple act of "conjuring" to Charlie.

After their explanation of the 1975 photographs, Rines and Wyckoff sat down to considerable applause. Now the two would watch the zoologists who supported the evidence do their stuff; like fakirs tiptoeing over hot coals, the experts rose to read their prepared statements. Said George Zug:

"The following statements represent my personal opinion. These statements do not represent an official view of the Smithsonian. The data gathered in 1972 consist of a 16-mm. film and a continuous sonar record. One part of the sonar record clearly shows a series of small objects and several larger objects. Sonar experts interpret the smaller

objects as fish and the larger objects as animate objects in the 20- to
30-foot size range. I concur with this interpretation and further
suggest that these are fish and the recently described *Nessiteras
rhombopteryx*, previously known as the Loch Ness monsters.

"Computer enhancement of the 16-mm. film frames taken at the
same time as the sonar record of large animate objects reveals a number of objects. The most distinct image is of a rhomboidal shape attached by a narrow base to a larger object. I interpret this as a flipperlike appendage protruding from the side of a robust body.

"The 1975 16-mm. film includes several frames containing images of
objects which possess symmetrical profiles, which indicate that they
are animate objects or parts thereof. I would suggest that one of the
images is a portion of the body and neck, and another a head.

"I believe these data indicate the presence of large animals in Loch
Ness but are insufficient to identify them. This new evidence on the
existence of a population of large animals in Loch Ness should serve
to encourage research on the natural history of Loch Ness and its plant
and animal inhabitants, and remove the stigma of 'crackpot' from any
scientist or group of scientists who wish to investigate the biological
and limnological phenomena in Loch Ness."

Other experts also presented statements generally echoing Zug's
belief that Rines' pictures showed a huge living creature. Besides Zug
there was Christopher McGowan, an associate curator in the Department of Vertebrate Paleontology at the Canadian Royal Ontario Museum. The mild, bearded McGowan would soon find himself on the
hunt for bones in the loch.

There were also statements from Roy Mackal, a pioneer monster-
hunter from the University of Chicago; from A. W. Crompton, a respected Harvard zoologist; from experts at the New England Aquarium; and, of course, the statements from the nonbelieving experts at
the British Museum of Natural History.

Rines had by no means been the first person mesmerized by the
idea of a giant beast in Loch Ness, and the next section of the
symposium in Parliament covered previous efforts to reveal the loch's
secret. The major effort had been by the British Loch Ness Investigation Bureau, a volunteer organization that had sponsored 10 years
of efforts to photograph the beast on the surface. David James, one of
the bureau founders rose to address the audience. He noted ironically
that in the 30,000 man-hours bureau volunteers had spent peering

across the puzzling surface of the loch, they were never able to improve on photographs of the beast taken the year before they began, in 1961, or the year after the project died, in 1971, for lack of funds. Rines' 1972 pictures had been obtained the year after the bureau suspended their expeditions. The year before the bureau began, an inadvertent film of a huge object surging across the loch launched monster-hunter Tim Dinsdale on his personal crusade to solve the strange mystery.

Tim Dinsdale had been an aeronautical engineer, drawn to the loch after becoming intrigued by the subject and analyzing the evidence. His studies of the old photographs purporting to be the monster's humps in the water, and of the accounts of eyewitnesses, convinced him that there was a large unknown animal in the loch. Carefully preparing himself with cameras and camping equipment, he set out on his first trip to the loch in April 1960. After only a few days at the loch, he had the luck—good or bad—to obtain the remarkable film. After that, he became a confirmed monster-hunter, throwing up his career to spend months at the loch, scanning the surface and waiting for the beast to appear.

Dinsdale showed to the audience in Parliament his grainy 30-foot strip of black-and-white film of a distant hump plunging through the calm waters of the loch, creating a large wake. After a few minutes of random zigzagging, the hump turned abruptly left and moved rapidly parallel to the opposite shore. Dinsdale told the audience he had even seen the animal's paddle strokes as it proceeded. Always the careful scientist, Dinsdale had later wisely sent out a 14-foot fishing boat along the same course, and filmed it for comparison. The boat could be clearly recognized as a boat and was quite different from the hump filmed earlier.

The film had created a popular sensation at the time, but was not considered a serious scientific threat until it came under analysis in 1966 by the RAF's Joint Air Reconnaissance Intelligence Center. This military unit, whose photoanalysis of aerial reconnaissance film had distinguished it during World War II, concluded that the object in Dinsdale's film was neither a surface boat nor a submarine, "which leaves the conclusion that it is probably an animate object," said the center's report. The experts concluded that the object's cross-section was not less than six feet wide and five feet high.

While Dinsdale's film was perhaps the most convincing photographic evidence of the beast's existence, Alexander Campbell was perhaps the most convincing witness of the thousands who have actually seen the beast. The next piece of evidence in the presentation in Parliament was a film of Campbell recounting his most interesting sighting. In his 45 years as "water bailiff," or game warden, the spare old Scotsman had experienced every animal and trick of light the loch could throw at him. But the tricks of the sun, the mists, and the common animals of the loch were sorted out and catalogued by experience, and Campbell is certain he has seen the beast many times.

His first sighting had been early one morning in May 1934. Campbell was standing at the mouth of the River Oich, which flowed past his door. Suddenly something seemed to shoot out of the water about 400 yards away, riveting his attention. In the film shown in Parliament, he stood beside the loch, recounting his experience.

"I saw it about 100 yards beyond a red pole and near the [Fort Augustus] Abbey boathouse," said Campbell. "This thing caught my attention early in the morning, bright sunny morning, flat calm. It had a long neck, like a serpentine neck, huge humped body, and a small head, and it seemed to be very timid and it kept turning its head this way and that. Well, it was swimming on the surface for several minutes, I should think, and I estimated the length at anything up to 30 feet from one end of the hump to the other; and the length of the neck above water level, I should say, was fully six feet."

As Campbell watched, the glistening dark gray hump and slender neck remained on the surface until the sound of engines intruded. Two small fishing trawlers slowly chugged into sight. The animal lowered its head and sank rapidly out of sight, shattering the mirror-stillness of the loch surface.

"So I didn't know what to say, I was so taken aback. I ran home, turned up the book on extinct prehistoric animals, and the nearest thing I could find in the book was the picture of the plesiosaur," said Campbell.

Dinsdale and Campbell were two archetypes of the enormous cast of characters who had encountered the beast. Dinsdale was "The-Man-Who-Gave-Up-Everything-for-His-Quest." Campbell was "The Experienced-Professional-Who-Knew-the-Loch." But there was a third category—"The-Average-Person-Who-Had-the-Hell-Scared-Out-of-Him"—into which fell most of the people who had seen the beast. This was the category of R. H. Lowrie, the next guest on the program in Parliament.

Lowrie was a businessman and pleasure yachtsman, who told the story of his 1960 sighting with an embarrassed puzzlement; he still suffered from the aftermath of the confusing, frightening experience:

"It was on an occasion in 1960 that we were proceeding about our lawful business going from one end [of the loch] to the other to get to the east coast, our home port, and we had one small boy on watch," said Lowrie. "The rest of us were having Sunday lunch down below because it was wet and rather calm and unpleasant, when he shouted down, 'There's something coming up the stern; does anyone know what it is?'

"At this point his mother thought it prudent to go to the cockpit to see what was going on. And, sure enough, coming up the stern, quite perceptibly and quite fast, was this phenomenon." It was, Lowrie wrote in his log, a curious green and brown form, occasionally submerging, with a necklike protrusion breaking the surface.

"We had a very good view of it and enjoyed seeing it. It went past and after it had gone past, someone said, 'We should have taken a picture of that.' And a great search was made, and to the credit of us all, a camera was found and a picture produced.

"After that, as we were nearing the Inverness end of the loch and our destination, which by this time my wife was rather keen to get into at the [canal] lock gate, this phenomenon returned and had the appearance of quite some size, causing us concern," said Lowrie. The large hump had reversed course, plowing back toward the now seemingly small craft.

"It returned on reciprocal course—i.e., it would have been on a collision course—at which point my wife said, 'Well, enough's enough, and home we're going, and better get the children off the deck and get into the lock and see that the lock keeper shuts the gates at night!'

"When we got into the [canal] lock, someone very kindly came along and said, 'We have seen you seeing what is known as the Loch Ness monster. If you'll take my advice you'll forget about it.' And, in fact I did, and if it hadn't been for the fact that Sir Peter Scott happened to know and ran the trace because of the number on our sail, we still never would have been found out. Really, quite frankly, I don't think I'd be awfully sorry."

What made Lowrie's sighting especially significant was that the beast had been seen independently by a party of watchers on land, including veteran monster-hunter Torquil MacLeod, who said he had seen two pairs of paddle splashes, the rear splashes twice the size of the front ones. This backup testimony made a powerful case that the sighting had not been a trick of light or a common animal misinterpreted.

Finally, after more reports of new sightings and discussions on legislation to protect the beast, the question-and-answer period of the symposium began. Throughout the symposium, the monster-hunters had wondered what the finale would bring. Expert zoologists had sat patiently in the dark hall biding their time until the monster-hunters had finished.

First came a swipe at the secrecy and turmoil surrounding the photographs, by Sir Humphrey Greenwood of the British Museum of Natural History. Greenwood vigorously and bluntly demanded a scientific publication:

"This is no forum in which for us to come to a conclusion!" said Greenwood. "I think the only conclusion we can hope to reach is that it must be published in great detail, with all the evidence from all the experts of Dr. Rines' team and everybody else who's contributed. There are all sorts of bits of evidence now scullying about, as it were, for the public to read. And I think these things have got to be gone into detail and refuted if they're not correct."

Then Gordon Sheals, Rines' chief scientific critic, began his attack on Rines' evidence. His mop of white hair setting him apart in the crowd, the old zoologist began politely and precisely, a touch of coldness tingeing his voice. He first suggested that the large flipper was actually a small fish fin photographed close up. Greenwood rose to back him up, intimating that he believed that the flipper picture could be the tail of a shark. A cloud began to form over the gathering. The British scientists were hinting that they believed the evidence was a hoax. But another scientist refuted the shark theory by pointing out that the flipper was clearly attached to a large body and not to a shark's slim tail section.

A professor at Kings College, Cambridge, rose to defend the British scientific community. "I take exception to the fact that one hears it being criticized this way. . . . I have always found British scientists willing to listen and consider evidence in a reasonable way. The evidence that has been presented tonight seems to me to add only a little—but significant little—to what has been known in the past." He further attacked the group for their lack of controls. Where were the shots of other, common loch animals? Where were other pictures that have been subjected to the mysterious, suspicious process of computer enhancement? The air was growing thick with accusation.

The questions and answers had been a gradual crescendo in the final movement of a symphony of accusation. Sheals rose to deliver the coda. Trembling with anger, he read his statement from a paper in his hand.

"It seems to me that there is no evidence whatsoever to support the view that the same object is featured in each of the photographs, and I think it is deceptive. There is no evidence to support the view that these objects are living animals, and neither is there any evidence at all to link the 1975 series with earlier photographs.

"Regretfully I have to say that it seems to me that the publication of an article describing and formally naming an animal thought to be represented in two of these photographs is unfortunate and regrettable.

"The allocation of a formal scientific name to the supposed animal is likely to convey to the layman a false notion of reality and objectivity. Scientifically, it can serve no useful purpose and has merely added to the clutter of dubious names already in the literature."

An unruffled Edgerton repeated his reasoning that led him to the inescapable conclusion that the flipper was gigantic. Said Edgerton: "It was in focus; it filled the camera frame. . . . To meet both criteria, it could only be about six feet long."

Peter Scott delivered a counterattack on Sheal's criticism: "I find very strange [the questioning of the flipper's size] to be made in such a blunt way by a careful scientist, a suggestion that we are wildly exaggerating, on a particular feature where we feel we have absolute evidence."

With this dramatic confrontation, the meeting was closed, and the antagonists left to think over what they had seen and heard. Science had progressed, but as usual the progress had been accompanied with pratfalls, stupidity, and misunderstanding, but with just enough logic to glue the mess together.

Sheals was *right*; Rines *had not* shown them the careful control shots of other, familiar objects under the loch, or the documented measurements, or evidence that the photographs were of the same object.

However, Sheals was also *wrong*; Rines *had* produced evidence that the photographs *were* of living animals. In two succeeding pictures, the 1972 flipper had moved and changed shape. At the same time the flipper shots were taken, the sonar showed large objects moving in front of the camera. The 1975 photograph of the head showed bilateral symmetry. The evidence was strong that in 1975 "underwater objects" had bashed the camera. The photographed shapes had shown up in one frame and vanished in the next, without reappearing, as might be expected with a floating log or the loch bottom.

Edgerton was certainly right; Doc, the instigator, wound up the symposium with a call to arms, as the flipper picture loomed above him on the screen.

"I think the thing I see in this picture is the inspiration to get into action and get some bigger film, better optics, better lighting," said Doc.

"To me it's a disappointment to spend all our time talking about poor pictures when the opportunities are there to get some marvelous things of this creature. This whole symposium to me is just inspiration to get on with the job and to get some more equipment!"

His call would be heeded.

◉ Chapter Three
THE PLAN

The meeting in Parliament was reported only lightly in the press, some believed because it had been held late in the evening, after the morning papers had gone to bed. Others believed the press had grown tired of the latest Loch Ness business. But the meeting had been useful for Rines. The British Museum of Natural History had at least asked for the material to be published so they could examine it thoroughly. And the British scientific journal *Nature* had noted Rines' progress in persuading the scientific world of his seriousness.

"If the eventual truth of the monster-hunters' claim is still breathlessly awaited," said *Nature*, "at least they, though perhaps not their prey, have finally come in from the cold. That may be the epitaph on this episode. In the next one, the natural history of Loch Ness may even become a respectable line of study."

Other magazines were not so circumspect. In the United States, *Time* was busy whipping up a frothy article designed to cast considerable doubt on Rines' credibility. In its January 12, 1976, issue, *Time* hinted that Rines and his academy were not on the up and up: "The [academy], which has no connection with any university or recognized research institution, is vague about its membership and seems to have financed little in the way of study on its own." (This was the same magazine that had called the academy a group with "apparently impeccable" credentials in a 1972 article about the flipper pictures.)

In the January 12 article, *Time* lumped several monster-hunters together, apparently trying to eke out a little guilt by association. Besides covering Rines, the article mentioned a fellow academy member who had hunted the Bigfoot of the Pacific Northwest and a lawyer unconnected with the academy who had purchased an unusual chimpanzeelike animal. Said *Time*: "An Academy member, Peter Byrne, has searched for the legendary Bigfoot. A New York lawyer has acquired an animal that some feel may even be Bigfoot. Michael Miller bought the creature, described as resembling a bald chimpanzee with an ear job and a sour disposition, from an animal show for $10,000."

Ignoring much of the evidence presented in Parliament, and the caliber of the men who presented it, *Time* served up every ring of the many-ringed circus that the controversy had become, including the fact that the letters in *Nessiteras rhombopteryx* could be rearranged to spell "Monster hoax by Sir Peter S." (In fact, the scientific name can also be rearranged to form "Yes, both pix are monsters. R." as well as many other anagrams.)

Prominent members of the British scientific community were certainly up in arms over the new controversy, angry at the circus the press had made out of the new evidence and also at Rines and his colleagues for—they believed—allowing it to happen. They were incensed at the secretiveness surrounding the evidence, wondering why it had not been published fully and openly to begin with. One well-known British scientist complained that Sir Peter Scott had approached him at a party, offering to show him Rines' pictures, hidden in Sir Peter's coat as if they were smutty French postcards.

Many scientists were suspicious of the motives of Rines and his colleagues, suspecting that they were merely hoaxers after money. There had been many such sensational photographs in the past purporting to show the beast that had later turned out to be the work of pranksters or con artists. The participation, however, of Dr. Edgerton —an internationally known and respected scientist—did much to quiet the suspicions about the honesty of Rines and others.

Of the possibility of a Loch Ness monster, some scientists stated flatly that Loch Ness had already been thoroughly explored and that no evidence of large creatures had been uncovered by official science. Others contended that the basic conditions for the existence of a colony of large reptiles—such as sufficient food supply and high water temperatures—did not exist. Rines' photographs, they said, could have been misinterpreted or faked. But always there was the sonar evidence of large objects moving under the loch. This was more difficult to explain away, and it silenced the more vocal objections, but still left the scientist's dissatisfied.

The damning press reports and scientific denunciations stemming from the new evidence weren't too bothersome to Rines; he had been attacked before. More important was the immediate necessity to publish his results. But where? Just as the beast had materialized in front of his camera in June 1975, so a magazine materialized that December. It was *Technology Review*, a combined technical journal and alumni magazine published at the Massachusetts Institute of Technology.

This was when I first got to know the monster-hunters. As managing editor of *Technology Review*, I had written Rines a letter proposing that the magazine publish a full scientific account of his findings, with his photographs in color, and allowing all the space he needed for explanation. This precisely fitted the directive Rines had received from the scientific establishment. The magazine also offered rapid publication—in the March/April 1976 issue—and Rines was certainly aware that publication in *Technology Review* would add credibility to his efforts because of its affiliation with M.I.T. Doc's affiliation with the Institute, as well as Charlie Wyckoff's and Martin Klein's, made publication in the *Review* all the more logical.

Throughout January and into February 1976, the pictures were made ready and a full account of the research was prepared. There were nervous moments for the magazine's editor, John Mattill. Was this project a hoax? Would the high command of M.I.T. come down on the magazine for publishing such far-out material? Although he remained uneasy, Mattill concluded that enough qualified people were involved for it not to be a hoax. And when news of the impending publication reached the M.I.T. administration, they assumed the wait-and-see attitude scientists should before the evidence is in.

Publication day was set for April 8, 1976, with a press conference in New York the evening before. The small hotel meeting room was packed for the conference, and they heard the same evidence Rines and Wyckoff had presented in Parliament in December. The *Technology Review* article contained all the photographs taken in 1972 and 1975, as well as careful explanations of the reasoning behind their analysis. It concluded with a ringing call to logic: "Although we make no claim to being expert zoologists, we can find no combination of phenomena that account for these data as well as the simple explanation that a large creature inhabits the loch. Not even the experts have offered a plausible alternative explanation, in our view," said the article.

"It is a philosophic rule that if a given set of data has more than one explanation, the true explanation is probably the simplest one. To put it another way, 'the shortest distance between two points is a straight line.'

"We submit that it is a patent violation of this rule to explain away our data, as well as the reputable historical data on the Loch Ness phenomenon as a complex series of mistaken sightings, equipment failures, artifacts, or hoaxes."

Perhaps the logic of the article was persuasive, or perhaps the magic of *Technology Review*'s printed pages had worked its charm. Whatever the case, a wave of more favorable publicity began. The first evidence was *The New York Times*' front-page story the next day, headlined "Loch Ness Monster: A Serious View," which soberly reported that reputable scientists were beginning to examine the Loch Ness evidence with respect. That evening Eric Sevareid on the "CBS Evening News" followed *The Times*' lead with the kind of rambling, navel-contemplating discourse that the beast has always seemed to inspire in journalists:

"The real question is: is Nessie reptile or fish?" he said. "The scientists will find out. They will get her because she is there, as Everest was climbed because it's there, as the other side of the moon was explored because it's there . . . mysteries are intolerable to many people. The tormented soul of a resigned president must be laid bare. Sex must be public. Nessie must be found, trapped, measured, and analyzed, and maybe she will end up at Disneyland performing twice a day, catching frozen fish in her mouth on cue."

Science News, another respected publication, said of the *Technology Review* article: "To their credit Rines and his colleagues have refrained from speculating about the identity of Nessie. . . . Yet the British museum zoologists choose to criticize the work along lines which none of *them* had expertise [questioning the photographic methods]." Other newspapers and magazines around the country reported the newly published results, with more or less accuracy, but with much more respect.

Months before the magazine's publication, Rines, Wyckoff, and Doc had already plunged into debate and planning for the 1976 expedition—the expedition to reveal the mystery once and for all! On January 5, 1976, the team sat down for dinner at Doc's apartment overlooking the Charles River near M.I.T. Together they tried to figure the best approach for capturing on film the creature in the loch 3,000 miles away.

Rines was exultant at having finally persuaded Doc to accompany him to the loch. Rines remembered the years of approaching the tough old scientist, and receiving equipment and advice, but no active participation. When the films from earlier, unsuccessful expeditions would be developed, an eager Rines and his wife Carol would head for Doc's cluttered office tucked away on an upper floor of M.I.T.'s main building. The blinds would go down, the lights turned off, and Bob and Carol would wax enthusiastic over their underwater photographs. Could that be the monster? What do you think that is? Gee, it looks like a fin! The two would rush excitedly up to the screen. Look at that! Could that be something?

Doc smiled knowingly, occasionally giving his secretary Jean a dig in the ribs. The Rineses would proclaim the amazingness of their pictures —of rocks, logs, fish—taken that summer in the murky loch. They were trying as much to keep up their own enthusiasm as to interest Doc.

But nothing on the films really excited Doc, so he remained encouraging but uncommitted. Even after the flipper shots in 1972, he still didn't feel the project fascinating enough to join an expedition to the loch. But the 1975 photographs changed things profoundly. Doc was certainly excited about the photographs of the creature, but perhaps more so about the photographs of the underside of the boat. Here was evidence that something large had bashed the camera about. Any beast that could knock a 75-pound camera-strobe system around was no will-o'-the-wisp—not a log that had floated in front of the camera, or a clump of algae that had contorted itself into a monstrous shape. None of those things—not even a human diver—had the power to knock into a vertical position such a heavy camera rig, suspended in the middle of 70 feet of water. Now, *there* was substance!

Doc joined Rines and Wyckoff, wholeheartedly, and in meeting after meeting in the spring of 1976, the concept of the new equipment came together. Each new camera, each new idea, was aimed at answering a criticism of the previous equipment. For instance, Sheals and other scientists had not trusted Charlie's measurements of the beast using light intensities and lines of shadow. Thus stereo cameras would be used so that measurements could be triangulated. Two underwater cameras, side by side, snapping simultaneous pictures, would offer incontrovertible proof that the beast was indeed huge, and not a gnat looming close to the cameras. Moving pictures would be even more convincing, so it was decided that the expedition would feature an underwater television camera aimed with the other cameras. It would allow the scientists to decide when to fire the stereo cameras and to make videotapes of what went on in front of the cameras. The videotape recorder could be operated at a slow, tape-conserving speed of one frame per second so that they could leave the recorder on at all times, even when no one was monitoring.

There were arguments over strategies. Rines was still enthusiastic about the idea of putting down a camera rig activated by a computer attached to sonar. Such a rig could hang in the loch indefinitely, without the need for constant observation. Then, when a large object intruded into the sonar beam, the camera could bang off pictures at a prodigious rate. The failure of such systems in the past had not deterred Rines. The idea of sonar activation was still valid. But Doc wanted to have a human decide when to press buttons and take pictures—to use "our God-given intelligence!" he would exclaim.

The three technologists were also intrigued that the beast in 1975 had actually swum in to hit the 16-mm. underwater camera. Was it attracted to the brilliant, periodic flash of light from the strobe? Or was it the high-pitched beep put out by the strobe light as it flashed? Or the electrical field induced in the water by the strobe's electrical system? Zoologists had told Charlie that many fish hunted their prey by sensing the electrical field generated by the prey.

Whatever the reason for the attraction, in 1975 the 16-mm. camera, Old Faithful, would serve as an effective "bait" for the creature, with the other cameras aimed at it. Thus, if something disturbed the bait camera, not only would it capture pictures of the episode, but the stereo cameras would take pictures of the bait camera's being disturbed. There would be all sorts of scientific controls and improved cameras this time. Even Old Faithful was to be powered this year by a line to shore, rather than by batteries. With ample shore power the strobe, thus, could probe further into the loch and could be an even more powerful homing beacon for the beast.

Although the "TV/stereo frame," as it was to be called, was their pride and joy, the engineers had developed other new cameras to be lowered into the waters of the loch. The silhouette camera was a small yellow cylinder to be suspended from a buoy and aimed upward, left to automatically click off pictures every five seconds or so during the daytime. Should the beast swim between the camera and the surface, the wide-angle lens would capture its silhouette, perhaps its entire body. For the first time, the monster-hunters would know the shape of the entire creature, not of just a flipper or a head. They would have a master plan of the beast and would be able to assemble the puzzle from the other photographic data.

The work on the silhouette camera led to the happy discovery of another camera expert who was interested in the mission—John Lothrop of Polaroid Corp. Charlie had needed help with the silhouette camera and called a friend at Polaroid. Soon John Lothrop, head of Polaroid's experimental model shop, showed up. He became so intrigued with the project that he proposed to develop an underwater Polaroid camera for the TV/stereo rig to give instant pictures of whatever passed in front of the bank of cameras. He set to work, not only developing his camera, but aiding with all the rest. The Polaroid SX–70 was ideal for taking finished pictures quickly; it produced developed pictures as fast as its button was pressed. The other cameras required a wait of several seconds between flashes; their strobe lights had to build up energy to discharge.

With Doc involved, equipment was readily loaned. From Sam Raymond, an old friend and president of the underwater camera company Benthos, Inc. came the loan of the stereo cameras. They had been designed for work on such projects as undersea oil drilling and pipeline inspection. From Doc's friends at the National Geographic Society came wide-angle lenses to be fitted on the Benthos cameras. Ike Blonder, a long-time colleague of Rines and an acoustic expert, donated the videotape recorder.

Doc had plenty of strobe lights in his lab, so he and Charlie and Bill MacRoberts, Doc's experienced technician, went to work to form the separate pieces into a working system.

Throughout March and April and into May 1976, they worked steadily in Doc's lab. It was a large old room crammed with electronic parts, underwater cameras, frames, wires, bolts—bits and pieces of every description. The comfortably cluttered place was festooned with peculiar relics from Doc's past adventures, hanging from the old water pipes crisscrossing the high ceiling—spear guns, tillers, sponges, huge light bulbs, even ears of corn.

Doc, Charlie, and MacRoberts, with Lothrop periodically joining in, solved a steady stream of problems, their deft fingers performing intricate tasks from bolting the camera frame together, to making electronic connections. As they worked, they talked out the many problems, asked questions, used the information, found the parts, fitted them on. The engineers possessed an experienced set of connections among brain, eyes, fingers, mouth. With Doc and Bill perched on stools at one end of the lab, and Charlie at the other, clambering about on a ladder next to the growing camera frame, they coaxed the equipment from plan to reality.

After sawing, bolting, thinking, fitting, they came up with a 10-foot-long metal frame which would support all the cameras. It consisted basically of two parallel steel bars, with supporting cross-members. The frame would hang vertically in the loch from a boat or floating platform, with the cameras mounted horizontally, all peering together out into the darkness. At the bottom of the frame were the two heavy steel stereo cameras, side by side; next up was the television camera, perched inside a gray plastic cylinder; and next up was the Polaroid camera also in a large plastic cylinder.

Bolted on the top portion of the frame, aimed outward and slightly downward, were the plastic cylinders containing powerful strobe lights to produce flashes of brilliant light for the cameras. There was also a large brown plastic cylinder containing flashbulbs for the Polaroid unit. A sheaf of black cables running up and down the frame electrically bound the system into a coherent whole.

These wires culminated in the cylinder housing the television camera, and from this camera, sprung a 300-foot-long black cable which would run from the camera frame hanging in the loch to a control hut on shore. At the other end of the cable, on shore, would be a television monitor and a small metal control box, fiddled together with parts from Doc's lab. The control box was fitted with two large old-fashioned counters to record how many photographs had been taken with the stereo and Polaroid cameras. A small ammeter on the control box told the operator if there was enough power to fire the cameras, which were run off batteries on shore.

The most exciting features of the control box, though, were the two little white buttons, one marked "stereo" and one marked "Polaroid." An operator sitting on the shore, pressing those buttons at the right time, could make history, taking the first clear underwater pictures of the beast. They were innocent-looking little buttons, but very tantalizing.

The camera system was an imposing mass of equipment. Should the beast dare to confront it, the cameras on the frame would wrest more information from the animal than decades of above-water photographs and the many excited descriptions by eyewitnesses. If the equipment was successful, the beast would be revealed in instant pictures, stereoscopic pictures, moving pictures, and would be seen by one flabbergasted human—the first person in history to confront the beast in its own element.

Besides the equipment, other promising developments added to the excitement over the 1976 expedition. John Noble Wilford, head science writer for *The New York Times* contacted Charlie with a proposal that *The Times* help sponsor the expedition. *The Times*, known as the "Gray Lady," was apparently ready to kick up her skirts a bit; she would give Rines and the Academy $20,000, and in turn would receive first newspaper rights to any pictures, a 24-hour head start on any major stories, and the sole rights for her reporter and photographer to go out in the research boats with the expedition members. As a side agreement, *The Times* proposed that it act as agent for all rights to the pictures.

Rines was delighted at the prospect of *The Times'* participation. Not only would the expedition's reputation be enhanced by reportage in *The Times*, but the money would help defray expenses, and *The Times* would take care of the dickering over rights. But Charlie was not so sure about the proposal; he disliked the idea of holding back news of the expedition for one news source, and he was dubious about having scientific results reported first in a newspaper. There had been trouble with the scientific establishment without this disregard of their esteemed scientific journals and symposia. But in the end Rines won out, and the Gray Lady donned boating sneakers and boarded the mission.

The expedition had a tight schedule to meet, which included not only assembling the equipment, but also testing it in the New England Aquarium in Boston. The first underwater test came on May 1, 1976, and it was of the camera Old Faithful, in its improved shore-powered version. There was a quiet sense of excitement around the aquarium's huge central tank as the camera and strobe system was assembled for lowering into the water. The scene was a lonely ghostly one, for few people were in the dark, cavernous building late at night. The walls around the top of the 30-foot tank were decorated with black silhouettes of the most dreaded monsters of the ocean—the sharks. It was a jarring realization that one of the largest of all sharks, the Great White, was only about 20 feet long—about half as big as some estimates of the beast in the loch.

Rines and Wyckoff crouched over the two yellow cylinders, attaching them to the metal frame, loading the film, and sealing the cylinders against leakage. They were both happy engineers; especially Rines, for his 1976 equipment would be much more elaborate than the beg-borrow-wheedle makeshift apparatus he once had to resort to. Still, the expedition was far removed from the multimillion-dollar government-financed research programs. There were still little instances of make-do. Rines used black electrical tape to seal the cameras and motorcycle straps to hold the cameras onto the frames. But the apparatus worked, and that was all that counted. At least the independence-loving Rines had the thrill of following a path of inquiry because he wanted to, and not because the government agreed that he should.

As they worked over the slightly battered camera, Rines was pensive. "I wish I could have seen what this camera has seen." It was a comment borne out of envy, but also of frustration at suffering such equipment limitations when there were such marvelous data to be had!

At last everything was ready; the camera was switched on and began taking pictures every 15 seconds, with click-wheeze sounds made by the shutter operating, followed by the film advancing. Charlie plugged in the strobe, and a brilliant flash joined the click-wheeze concerto.

Sharks, turtles, and other large sea creatures circled in the lighted pool as Rines and Wyckoff lowered the metal frame supporting the yellow cylinders. I had joined them for the first test, and together we watched intently to see how the captive animals in the tank would react to the camera. Would they attack? Flee? Have a strobe light for lunch? Their relationship to the camera would give some hint of what the beast in the loch might have felt toward the yellow intruders in 1975. The huge sea turtles were the first to respond to the cameras, with a fluid curiosity. One by one they would glide up to the suspended cylinders, eye them coldly, nudge their way around them, take a few halfhearted nips, and then swim away, their curiosity satisfied.

The sharks and most of the other fish seemed indifferent to the flashing, clicking, electrified machines. The blinding flash of the strobe made little difference to them when they happened to be caught in front of the light.

But the bluish trigger fish, with their tough coral-nibbling teeth, were entranced by the cylinders. They hovered around the frame constantly pulling and biting at it. We watched them closely trying to understand the reasons behind their interest. They hovered only behind the camera—not in front of it or near the strobe. It seemed to be the periodic click-wheeze sound that they liked, but who could know?

As he watched Old Faithful snapping off shots of the aquarium fish, Rines said he could almost taste the final victory of identifying the beast in the loch; he did not seem bitter about the past accusations and sarcasm toward him and his guest; he enjoyed only a pure exultation. He invited all who wished to join in the hunt; the zoologists, the press and all those who had questioned his reputation, his sanity, his motives. We left the camera clicking away amidst the creatures of the aquarium, certain that at least one piece of equipment would work well.

The next day the unit was hauled back up, the salt water of the aquarium washed off, and the film unloaded. Old Faithful had taken beautiful pictures; hundreds of calibration shots of known fish, so that zoologists could not accuse the monster-hunters of foisting a fish fin off on them as the flipper of the beast.

The plans, the equipment, and the sense of excitement had all begun to gather momentum by the May 15, 1976, grand meeting of all the expedition members. The meeting was appropriately held in a classroom near Doc's lab on the M.I.T. campus. If any institution was most responsible for the expedition, it was the Massachusetts Institute of Technology, although there was no formal connection between the two. The Institute's campus, stretched imposingly along the bank of the Charles River, across from Boston, had harbored most of the expedition members during their student days, including Rines, Wyckoff, Klein, and even Doc. It was at M I.T. that Rines had been instigated to form an expedition to the loch at the "First Monster-Hunting Seminar," sponsored by Doc in 1970. Roy Mackal and another monster-hunter, Robert Love, had told of their expedition plans then. And finally, M.I.T. was important because it was the cachet of the Institute, of the article in *Technology Review*, and of Doc's participation, that had attracted *The Times* to the expedition.

With the monster-hunters seated a bit incongruously in the venerable classroom's old wooden student desks, Rines began the meeting by reading a letter from Joseph Judge, one of the editors of *National Geographic*, who had attended that early meeting in which the *Geographic* had been shown the 1975 pictures.

Judge had later given a magazine interview in which he was quoted as commenting disparagingly on Rines and the photographs. His letter to Rines charged that his remarks had been distorted and that he was still firmly interested in and encouraging toward Rines and his hunt.

"I now know what it feels like to be bitten by whatever evil spirit inhabits the Loch Ness situation," Judge had written, vowing thenceforward to avoid talking to journalists about the beast.

Rines had received many such letters from various scientists deploring past incidents, wishing luck for the future, and, incidentally, hinting at interest in a piece of the monster-pie. *The National Geographic*, in fact, was busy organizing its own expedition to the loch, one that would avoid the problems of publicity altogether by pretending that its expedition was not really meant to photograph the monster—they were there to do a "general" survey of the loch for an article. The strategy was known as "keeping a low-low profile."

John Noble Wilford, science editor for *The Times* attending the meeting, was introduced by Rines. Wilford, quiet and reserved, sat in a corner witnessing the events, as his photographer ranged about the room. I was introduced as the press officer, deputized to act as a buffer between the expedition and the press, which had gained a reputation as voracious, unprincipled, and irresponsible. An element of paranoia had sprouted in the expedition, nurtured by Rines' past experience with the press, and the restrictions of the agreement with *The Times*.

There were security measures to be taken. Rines designated Charlie as "keeper of the films." I was to fend off the hordes of press the group expected at the site. We were all to keep our mouths tightly shut. Charlie began to feel the pressure as keeper, for after pictures of the beast were obtained, it was his responsibility to begin the whole chain of events that would lead to the release of the story to the world. He was worried about spies on the premises, posing as locals hired to run boats, etc. And if information leaked out, would the expedition members be held responsible? Would there be a firing squad, or merely a short period of hanging by the thumbs? It was a far different atmosphere from the almost devil-may-care attitude that had characterized the past expeditions. Now monster-hunting had become big time, and perhaps not as much fun as before.

There were even political factors to the expedition. The beast was Scottish, and we were Americans and Canadians. Rines warned that there could be xenophobic British worries that we would usurp the beast for Old Glory; so we had to ensure that there were British faces in the expedition crowd. Fortunately, scientists from British universities had become interested in the project, as well as Sir Peter Scott, Tim Dinsdale, and other old friends. Rines also urged the expedition members to be especially prim and proper while at the loch. Instances of rowdiness and dishonesty by other groups had incurred the displeasure of local residents. The friendship of the natives was, in fact, vital to the success of the mission, because from them would come tips on where to find gear, information on local conditions, and reports of where the monster had been sighted.

The local governmental organizations also had to be considered. The Highland Regional Council guarded the environment around Loch Ness; the expedition had to remain friendly to its members, who would monitor the activities of the expedition to assure that the community interests were served. As the monster had become more popular, they also had to assure that boats entering the loch were carefully monitored to see that there were no harpoons or explosives on board. There might be attempts to kill or capture one of the beasts. At the mention of this possibility, the name of Roy Mackal was brought up. The pioneer monster-hunter, a biochemist at the University of Chicago, still had dreams which made the expedition members uneasy, of capturing the beast in a huge cage—little-boy fantasies of the Great Triumph. The engineers feared that if one of the beasts was captured and died from the handling, the entire population could be wiped out. For instance, what if the dead beast was the only male or the only female? At the least, such a death would reduce the herd's reproductive viability.

Layer upon layer of human complication continued to pile upon the pure technological tasks of stalking the beast. The new evidence for the beast had to be not only scientifically sound, but also politically, psychologically, and environmentally sound. Only then would the beast be truly "discovered."

The meeting at M.I.T. continued, with Doc and Charlie describing the apparatus they had developed to photograph the beast, and then the first news from Christopher McGowan and Martin Klein on the planned sonar search for bones on the bottom. The sonar equipment used would be the most advanced available; so advanced, in fact, that it wasn't on the market yet. Klein had designed and built a sonar system that could better analyze and display the reflected sonar signal from the bottom. It could also simultaneously penetrate the bottom silt with a sonar beam aimed directly downward beneath the sonar fish, besides the two beams aimed out to either side. With this bottom-penetrating beam, the sonar experts could investigate the structure buried beneath the silt of objects lying on the bottom.

But regardless of how advanced Klein's "three-channel sonar" was, it would be useless if there were no animal bones to be found, or if the searchers couldn't detect the bones with sonar in the first place.

Christopher McGowan reported a gratifying success on detecting the bones with sonar. Charles Finkelstein, an engineer and diver working for Klein, had deposited a string of mastodon bones, which McGowan had carted in from Canada, on the bottom of a New Hampshire lake. He and Finkelstein had towed the sonar fish over the area in an attempt to relocate the bones and had detected them easily on the sonar record. Finkelstein displayed to the expedition members the paper chart showing a line of tiny dots representing the array of bones. It was a good omen in an otherwise admitted long-shot search. All the sonar team members realized that single bones would be indistinguishable from rocks, but skeletons would be recognizable from the patterns they evidenced. It was the jackpot—an intact skeleton—or nothing.

McGowan also depended on two other assumptions in the sonar search: that a dead animal sank, its skeleton remaining intact in one place, and that the beast had bones in the first place. McGowan was fairly certain that the animals sank when they died, that the loch "never gave up its dead." Forensic scientists who had worked in Scotland told him that the loch waters were so cold that any dead animal—or human drowning victim—in the loch would become waterlogged and sink before bacteria could begin rotting the carcass to produce buoying gases. Since the loch was so deep, the carcass could sink into depths at which any bubbles that did form in the carcass would be squeezed down, preventing them from buoying the carcass. Once a body was down in the loch, it was down, to be devoured by eels and other scavengers. Thus the bodies of the dead beasts—or at least their skeletons—should still rest on the bottom of the loch where they were deposited at death.

McGowan's second assumption was more hope than knowledge— that the beast had bones in the first place. Some monster enthusiasts believed that the creature was a giant worm and thus had no hard skeleton. If the animal was an invertebrate, not only would McGowan's hunt be useless, but the possibility of proving the monsters' existence would be set back considerably; for many zoologists would never be satisfied "until they had a bit of bone in their mitts," said McGowan.

The heaviest responsibility for the sonar search for bones—at least for the first month or so—would fall on Charlie Finkelstein, as would the harrowing responsibility of diving to investigate carcasslike objects detected by the sonar. Finkelstein was an expert diver, built like a sumo wrestler, and with an outward confidence bordering on brashness. But he was worried about the prospects of diving in a loch where an unknown animal the size of a house trailer could be lurking nearby.

Finkelstein knew that other divers—experienced professionals—had seen and felt strange things under the loch and had vaulted to the surface trembling with fright, resolving never to dive in the loch again. He knew of the two divers in 1970 who had been working underwater in Urquhart Bay at the same time Klein's sonar had detected the huge moving objects underwater. The divers were ascending together, far above the bottom, arms linked, when suddenly all four of their flippers touched something simultaneously. They had left the water forthwith.

In the Loch Ness Investigation Bureau's 1971 expedition, diver "Brock" Badger also had a frightening experience underwater. He had been swimming about underwater, enjoying the loch, after having helped place moorings on the bottom. Peering through the murky water, he had been frightened half out of his wits by a large featureless cylindrical object, about six feet in diameter, moving in front of him. He had burst to the surface, splashed to shore as fast as he could go, and had refused to swim in the loch again. The normally cheerful young Scotsman was quiet for days, and at first would tell his friends only, "I thought I saw something underwater."

The night after the meeting at M.I.T., Finkelstein dreamed of riding the beast—a glorious, perilous underwater trip astride the animal. It was a way to cope with the darkness of the future. He alone, of the expedition members, would go into the cold waters that were the beast's environment. The loch and the beast were both unknown, unpredictable. The beast was, in a very real sense, a creature from an alien world, as are all water creatures to humans. They breathe a different fluid. They are subject to different laws of gravity, of sensory experiences, of heat and cold. Finkelstein in his many dives had encountered some of the alien creatures the sea supported, and he knew enough to be respectful and properly wary of their whims. He would be a careful diver.

Klein next rose to speak to the expedition members—as excited about the prospects of exercising his sonar scanners as he was about finding the beast.

"Working with sonar just all kinds of impossible things always happen, and Loch Ness is one of those places. We're trying to learn how to improve our odds in this business, and Loch Ness just happens to be a fascinating place; the bottom's fascinating, the water column's fascinating. . . . I got longer sonar ranges in Loch Ness than I've ever gotten anywhere else. . . ." Normally Klein could see only about 600 to 900 feet with his sonar. But in Loch Ness the beam of sound had reached up to 2,400 feet. At times the sonar team could tow their fish down the center of the loch and pick up both sides at once. Klein believed that the phenomenon was due to the loch's low magnesium sulfate content, a chemical which is said to be a major attenuator of sound underwater.

Thus far, the meeting at M.I.T. had heard plans to see the beast with light and with sound waves, but George Newton, an M.I.T. professor at the meeting planned to use the creature's infrared—or heat—emanations to pinpoint it. Newton was one of many professionals with bright ideas attracted to the expedition after Rines had published his pictures. Newton knew that over the past few years supersensitive detectors had been developed to "see" infrared radiation. They had been used in Vietnam to see enemy soldiers by their body heat, and in the detection devices in high-flying spy planes. Newton proposed to borrow one of the new units, place it at a spot overlooking the loch, and try to detect the heat from a beast surfacing for air. Even if the animal were cold-blooded, he reasoned, it would still be warmer than its surroundings because of the internal heat from its muscles. If the animal were air-breathing, even if it breathed through the "horns" in the 1975 head photograph—barely dappling the surface—he would be able to detect it. The detector he planned to use could measure a temperature difference as small as one-tenth of a degree Centigrade. But first he would have to test his theory with objects in the loch, and this would be his purpose in the new expedition.

Newton concluded his presentation and an excited chatter among the expedition members began. There were no bad thoughts pervading the meeting. All was positive, the theories were beautiful, and optimism was the mood. But far offstage waited the expedition's quarry. As if to ward off bad luck, the technologists had never mentioned the beast throughout the meeting. A stranger would have had little idea what the expedition was seeking. But the beast was there in everybody's head; the tantalizing, horrible, exciting, fabulous animal that they had all set out to bring to bay. The meeting adjourned into an afternoon of planning and debating.

Over the past weeks, Rines had painstakingly gone over the plans for the expedition. He was certain that he had used all the lessons learned in six frustrating years at the loch to perfect the 1976 effort. He remembered those past forays only too well. On his first expedition to Loch Ness in 1970, he had learned, thanks to Klein's sonar, that there were large underwater moving objects, and that they did come into Urquhart Bay, a prime search area. He had also learned that the creatures were apparently immune to blandishments of food and sex, after spending the summer pumping various tempting smells and sounds into the loch. His friends in various scientific establishments had supplied him with a number of chemical extracts. There were extracts of sex glands of eels, sea cows, sea lions; there were substances known to attract fish; there were substances such as salmon oil, that smelled like fish; and there were tapes of various sea animal sounds to be fed into underwater speakers. Tantalizing disturbances did occur in the waters during the tests, but the results were generally negative.

On that first expedition, Rines, Dinsdale, and the other monster-hunters also experienced the typically odd, inexplicable incidents that had always maintained an atmosphere of tension on loch expeditions. One day, with Rines and Dinsdale in the boat, Ike Blonder, an expedition member and acoustic expert, was lowering a hydrophone into the loch to try to detect sounds of the beast. The boat was positioned smack in the middle of a large area of 600-foot-deep water.

Blonder had lowered the hydrophone to about 200 feet when its downward progress was abruptly blocked by something solid. The hunters looked at each other wide-eyed, too excited to speak. For what seemed like an eternity, they listened to the sounds of the hydrophone bouncing and rasping over the large obstruction, before it finally continued its descent unhindered to around 600 feet. The hydrophone could not have encountered an underwater ledge—the sides of the loch drop precipitously from the shores, and there are no underwater shoals. Neither are there fish big enough to cause such an obstruction, and logs simply do not suspend themselves underwater. Rines knew very well what the hydrophone had struck.

On the next expedition, in 1971, Rines learned he could take pictures under the loch. It was the first year he had borrowed Old Faithful, the elapsed-time camera, from Doc. During that expedition, Rines doodled the camera over the loch bottom, capturing various pictures of rocks, logs, fish, and weeds. But no beast, although one picture of a monster-like object on the bottom haunted Rines. Even though Doc had said it was a log, Rines was fascinated by how much the picture looked like the outstretched head and neck of the beast. He persisted in introducing beastlike features into his written descriptions: "Is it a log or ledge partly buried in the sand, shaped like a long neck, head, open mouth, eye, and bonelike elements in front?" he wrote in a report on the expedition.

In 1971, as always, the strange occurrences continued. Late one evening, Rines and some friends had lowered Old Faithful, flashing away, onto the bottom of a shallow area in Urquhart Bay, to take pictures overnight. Attached to the camera with long ropes were two large red buoys and a yellow one, to ensure that the camera would not be lost. Early the next morning one of the team members passed the area on the way to pick up Rines at his hotel and saw that the buoys were gone. He arrived at the hotel and congratulated Rines on having gone out so early to recover the gear. But Rines hadn't! They raced for the loch, discovered the buoys missing, and began scouring the shore, scanning the surface of the loch, and diving and grappling for the cameras beneath it.

They decided to prepare Doc for the worst, and after contacting the local constable, sent him a cryptic cable: "One sighting. Part of equipment stolen. Police helping." The next cable would inform Doc that it was *his camera* that had been stolen.

The camera had been almost given up for lost when one of the Loch Ness Bureau's boats, returning to its port, suddenly spotted the brightly colored buoys, floating in the middle of the loch, with the camera still attached. Rines eagerly had the film in the camera developed and discovered that the camera had been underwater during at least 11 hours of movement, in which it had ended up three miles away from its original mooring spot, against wind and current. As the camera was being dragged along, it was facing downward and backward, so it failed to capture on film what it was attached to. But there were occasional shots of the mooring ropes, trailing away into the gloom, perhaps looped around some vague shape in the distance. It could have been fishermen playing a trick, but Rines knew very well what had kidnapped his camera.

The 1971 expedition also marked the evaporation of any personal doubts Rines had about the beast's existence. This was the year he actually saw the beast himself. Before 1971, Rines had firmly believed in the thousands of consistent, reliable accounts of monster sightings that had occurred over the years. But to really convince him, there was nothing like a personal sighting, and Rines' came on June 23, 1971.

It was a pleasant Scottish dusk, and he was out with his wife Carol visiting two local residents, Basil and Winifred Cary. They were enjoying the view of the loch from the Carys' house across Urquhart Bay from Temple Pier when they saw a large hump emerge across the bay near Temple Pier. The hump moved slowly out into the loch, and the group watching it raced down toward the loch to get a better view. They passed a spyglass from one to another, examining the hump carefully, and agreed that there was a solid hump there, and it was about 20 feet long and about six feet high; they compared its size with that of a 53-foot fishing boat anchored nearby and agreed that it could be nothing but a living creature. The hump slowly turned, headed back into the bay, and submerged. The sighting was over and, as with so many others who had seen the humps, Rines had become mesmerized by his experience. The memory would never leave him; he had to know what was under the loch. A year later, he mentioned his sighting to a local farmer, Alex MacLeod. The old man had asked if it was about ten o'clock in the evening! Yes, said Rines.

Was it on June 23? Yes. MacLeod told Rines he had seen the hump, too. He had been fishing in one corner of the bay that evening and had witnessed the animal surfacing for the first time in his many years on the loch.

The 1972 expedition for a now-avid Rines was a year for realizing how many stubborn unbelievers existed. This was the year he obtained the flipper photographs, which together with the simultaneous sonar trace, convinced Rines that he finally had evidence to show the world. But the world didn't want to see it. The British Museum of Natural History released a statement saying the photographs were genuine, but they couldn't identify the creature attached to the large moving object. The pictures were published in a few newspapers and magazines, and the sonar evidence generally ignored. The remarkable pictures—the triumphant, formidable evidence Rines thought he had obtained— died a quiet death. It was the same fate that Rines had seen befall Tim Dinsdale's film even after scientific analysis had confirmed its validity.

For the next two years Rines was to learn lessons about the vagaries of the loch and of the people around it. In 1973 he discovered that the loch was cold, or rather that the cold water could affect his cameras. He had developed his ingenious camera system with the attached computer-monitored sonar beam watching the area in front of the camera. It was a lovely apparatus that could sit and wait passively as long as it took for the creature to swim by. But the camera Rines used was of a type not meant to be operated underwater; the grease inside the mechanism congealed in the cold water, Rines believed, and the constipated camera obtained no pictures. In 1973, however, Rines did have one triumph. He persuaded Charlie Wyckoff to go along with him, in return for helping Charlie on one of his adventures, to film an eclipse in Africa. That was the year Charlie became hooked on monster-hunting.

In 1974 Rines returned again, this time with a better sonar-activated rig, only to have it ruined by inept handling. The local barge company, hired to lower the concrete-based camera to the bottom, unceremoni-ously dropped the precious apparatus upside down onto the bottom of Urquhart Bay, where it was crushed beneath the concrete-weighted base.

The next year, on the triumphant 1975 expedition, Rines learned that the loch had a silty bottom. This time his ingenious sonar rig made it safely to the bottom, and during its month-long stay was triggered many times by a large underwater object but was blinded by silt stirred up from the bottom. Rines knew very well what had done the stirring.

But now it was 1976—a new year, new people, new equipment, and new enthusiasm. The May 15 meeting had been an invigorating success, and finally, on May 19 the *pièce de résistance* of the expedition— the TV/stereo camera frame—was ready for testing in the aquarium tank. It was a cool, spring night when the 10-foot-long steel frame and several cartloads of accompanying equipment were gingerly trundled out of Doc's lab, into his van, and down winding Boston streets to the aquarium.

Doc was delighted with the prospect of fiddling with the cameras. As we rode the aquarium freight elevator up with the equipment, he took off his battered felt hat. Happily, he donned a jaunty red stocking cap; a diving cap presented to him by none other than Madame Cousteau, wife of Jacques Cousteau. We knew then the expedition had truly begun.

We unloaded the electronic equipment from the carts. The sharks, turtles, and other denizens of the aquarium circled the huge lighted tank, waiting silently as before. Their unusual beauty was heightened by the gloom of the huge blue-lit concrete building around the tank.

The frame was massive, and it took careful, slow handling to avoid smashing one of the watertight camera cylinders or ripping out one of the myriad of connecting wires. Finally the frame lay balanced on the edge of the tank, ready to be lowered into the water. Jean Mooney found a champagne bottle, filled it with fresh Boston water, and we held a short christening ceremony as Rines happily poured the water over the frame. Slowly the frame was lowered into the tank, the gleaming cameras disappearing one by one beneath the surface. The team members leaned over the railing to watch for the bubbles that would signify leaks in the cameras.

As the frame poked into their world, the fish altered their monotonous circling of the tank only slightly to allow for the intruder. Doc sat with a tableful of control boxes off in a corner watching the TV monitor. He could see the fish perfectly as they approached the camera. Once satisfied that everything was in order, he began pressing the buttons, taking pictures of the fish he saw on the monitor. The fish were inundated by the brilliant flashes of light, but as usual they seemed not to mind in the least. Again, the feisty little trigger fish moved in, worrying the wires with their teeth, attacking the intruder.

As we watched those familiar ocean monsters swim in and out of the camera's view, we wondered how the reality of the beast of Loch Ness could ever be doubted. We were used to—even bored by— animals as fabulous and amazing as any Loch Ness monster. There were the huge sea turtles, carrying their own natural armor plate evolved through millions of years of genetic trial and error. And, of course there were the sharks—a mouthful of teeth and a blind appetite —which had been successful predators, for hundreds of millions of years. The sharks we watched gliding around the camera were practically identical to those which had swam in ancient waters inhabited by prehistoric reptiles. Had the great-great-great-etc. grandfather of one of these sharks encountered the ancestor of the beast of the loch?

After about an hour, Doc had flashed off all the stereo pictures, and the frame was hauled up and washed off. The next day Charlie developed the stereo pictures and found that they would constitute excellent evidence. One could view them side by side with a dual magnifying glass and see lifelike three-dimensional scenes. But more important, with three dimensions, one could obtain more precise measurements of the subject. And the two pictures combined to allow the viewer to pick out many more details than in each picture individually. In a typical individual picture, only about 25 fish were visible, but in the same pictures in a stereo pair almost twice as many could be picked out.

Since the Polaroid camera had not been on the camera frame for the first test, the technologists decided to test the main frame again a few days later. The second test was a totally different experience. NBC television had just signed on to do a documentary on the expedition, and the media circus atmosphere we were to encounter had begun. We had become news.

The bright lights, television crew, and cables strung throughout the aquarium had completely dispelled the eerie quality of the aquarium present in the previous tests; in its place was a feeling of confusion. There were crowds everywhere. Crowds carrying equipment into the aquarium, crowds setting it up, crowds putting it in the water, crowds watching the underwater television. A cocktail party in the lower reaches of the aquarium moved upstairs to watch us work. The party people crowded around, fascinated by the lights, the cameras, the scientists and the equipment. It was quite a spectacle. There was the television crew filming a staid, sober Doc intently fiddling with the controls, and peering over his shoulder, a slightly tipsy, tall, flashy fellow in a bright silk shirt, with a drink in his hand.

There was a sharp contrast between what the underwater cameras witnessed during this test and what they would soon see. At the aquarium were the lights and melee of the television crew filming the submerged camera frame and the blank, primitive eyes of the captured creatures. But 3,000 miles away were the quiet, cold lonely depths of Loch Ness, where it was late afternoon, and where lay the animal for whom all the fuss was being made.

⚜ Chapter Four
THE EXPEDITION

By May 30, 1976, the 2,000 pounds of equipment for the expedition
had been carefully packed and shipped ahead, and it was time for the
main contingent of the expedition to head for Scotland.

The first wave of the expedition from Boston consisted of Bob and
Carol Rines and their 18-month-old son Justice; Doc and Esther Edger-
ton, Charlie and Helen Wyckoff, John Wilford, and me and my wife
Joni and our two-year-old daughter Wendy. Marty Klein, Charlie
Finkelstein, and John Lothrop would follow later.

The departure was anything but auspicious. Pan Am flight 54 was
three hours late, and it wasn't until midnight that we were ready to
board for the overnight flight. The cavernous, dark terminal, with
knots of tired, depressed travelers standing about, seemed light-years
from the exotic loch. There seemed so much to overcome in getting
there. Once on board, we were scattered throughout the plane, further
dampening the excitement we had felt over the past week. But Rines
and the other were irrepressible. They commandeered an isolated bank
of seats at the front of the plane and resumed planning for the expedition as the jet vaulted out over the Atlantic—a fitful sleep eventually
came, with dreams of monsters and foreign lands, and Scottish lochs.

We were flying east toward the sun, so after a few hours it was an
unnaturally quick, almost explosive dawn that flooded light into the
small windows of the plane. Even though the expedition members
had been sleeping soundly, the light was irresistible. A primordial re-

action to the dawn brought us to life, stretching and yawning, and ready for a new day, even though our body rhythms told us it was still late at night. The ocean far below was barely visible, dotted with tiny whitecaps. It was an entrancing thought that we could well be flying over the very beasts we were hunting in the loch. In fact, if one did postulate the existence of the Loch Ness monster, one would have to also postulate the existence of the same creature in the oceans. The loch had been attached to the ocean until only a few thousand years ago; it had not been an isolated lake long enough for any form of life to evolve within it.

After a day of rest in London, our trip to the loch resumed when we boarded the airplane for Inverness, the largest city in the area. The prop-driven plane seemed to send us back in time. We were in the 1940s again, skimming noisily just above the cloud tops. Late in the evening we arrived at Inverness airport, a few strips of runway and a small modern terminal building set amidst an overwhelming splendor of rolling green countryside. But it was still light, for days in Scotland in the summer are about 21 hours long. The almost constant daylight disrupted our time sense, adding to the dreamlike quality of our time at the loch. A cool, light mist blanketed the straight, narrow roads as we drove into Inverness. We suddenly went abruptly from the 1940s back into the 1800s period of peasant farms. Along the road were small stone farmhouses looking like white eggs set in the greenest Easter-basket grass. They were constantly scoured clean by the rains, and the smoke of their chimneys was swept quickly away by the winds. Cows and sheep were dotted about the hillsides, as if arranged by a rather unimaginative artist for his painting.

Before we had a chance to get used to the 1800s, we lurched back another three centuries as a massive stone castle came into view. Sitting on a hill above the road, its windows boarded up, the castle's turrets were pierced by vertical slits for firing arrows, its thick front door ready to repel the sharp axes of attackers. Visions of dungeons, knights, broadswords . . . dragons.

Then we were in Inverness which sat at the head of Loch Ness, between the loch and the North Sea. All the time periods swirled together anachronistically: nestled happily side by side were ancient castles, cozy stone houses with chimneypots, new gas stations, old railroad stations, narrow streets, traditionally kilted Scotsmen and mod adolescents in gigantic platform shoes and hip-tight bell-bottomed pants.

After only an hour in northern Scotland, I believed it entirely possible that a prehistoric creature could have wandered into this confusing amalgam of times. It would have thrived, welcomed magnanimously in this enchanted, chronologically promiscuous place.

We drove quickly through the town and once again into the rich countryside. As we traveled through the farmland, the loch appeared on the left of the road as a deceptively modest River Ness, which widened to a calm inlet harboring pleasure boats. Next came Lochend, a clustering of white cottages on a white beach looking down the length of the long, narrow loch.

And then, blam! Loch Ness! The road arched upward, clinging to the narrow ledge blasted out of the mountainside. To the left, Loch Ness spread out below, a wide sheet of water terminated abruptly by a wall of mountains on the other shore. As the road curved around the steep cliffs, the loch was sometimes gloriously visible and sometimes tantalizingly hidden behind the screen of trees growing on the slope below the road.

The Great Glen holding Loch Ness is a huge gash in the earth's crust, filled with water millennia ago. The winds funnel between the walls of the glen like the air through a whistle, building up speed and force, often so violently that whitecaps mark the loch's surface. But as we drove by, there were no whitecaps, only small wavelets, with rolling mists hugging the surface of the water. The surface of the loch is featureless. There are no islands, no shoals, no jutting rocks to relieve the drama. It is an overpowering absoluteness. It was late, but a wan light still penetrated the gray mists, enough to give color to the rich, green foliage. The road was bordered with a thick covering of grass and wildflowers, and both along the road and clinging to the cliffs were the thick evergreens called gorse, bearing bright yellow flowers.

The trip down the loch was climaxed by the appearance of Urquhart Bay, a huge bite out of the loch's straight shoreline. Across the bay lay smooth, lush slopes where sheep grazed and at a promontory on the opposite side, sat Urquhart Castle, ruined and ominous. The castle would be a constant backdrop to the work at Temple Pier on our side of Urquhart Bay. It would be another nagging anachronism in the 20th-century world of cameras and sonar.

As the road wound away from the loch and toward the little village of Drumnadrochit, we could see the dense underbrush on the low marsh where the rivers Enrick and Coiltie ran into the bay. It was in Drumnadrochit, this town of white stone cottages, that many of the expedition members were to stay. Some of us stayed in the Drumnadrochit Hotel, a rich old 16th-century manor, while others lodged in private homes that offered "bed and breakfast" for a modest fee. Rines and his family would live in a cottage a mile up the mountain, from which he could see miles of the loch's surface, and Doc and Charlie and their wives stayed next door, at the house of local landowner Gordon MacKintosh. From these home bases we would hunt the beast.

The next morning, after a formal breakfast in the hotel dining room served by crisply dressed maids and kilted men; Joni, Wendy and I hiked down the narrow highway along the loch, and up the winding mountain road to Rines' cottage. The narrow lane was hemmed in on either side by trees, bushes, and lichen-covered rock ledges. The frequent rains, volcanic soil, and almost constant summer light produced lush vegetation.

We reached Rines' cottage and the attached garage that was to be used as a workshop, and we turned to look back at the way we had come. An enthralling view of the loch stretched out below. The sun streaming through the clouds played over the loch and the mountainsides on the opposite shore. An occasional abrupt shaft of light would pierce the clouds and spotlight a portion of water or earth. Urquhart Castle rose from the opposite side of the bay, its ruined tower lit by the rays of the morning sun.

But the most fascinating part of the loch was its surface. Standing in the morning light, watching the loch, we came to understand why the beast had remained hidden for so many centuries. The waters of the loch surface protected it by displaying incredible patterns of ripples, waves, light and shadow to confuse the eye and cast doubt on sightings. Waves seemed to hover in one spot; sinuous patterns of ripples stirred by a breeze would skitter across the wide expanse of water; dark splotches seemed to move under the loch; patches of calm could mark something large swimming just beneath the surface. When a boat passed, its wake would reflect off the shore of the narrow loch and return to meet the wave from the opposite shore, setting up a train of traveling waves that numerous eyewitnesses had taken for a many-humped creature. Because there was such a vast stretch of water visible in any one place there was always a myriad of surface patterns to fascinate the viewer.

Doc and Charlie, however, ignored the scenery, being hard at work in the garage that morning. They had much to do. While Doc set up the television gear for testing, Charlie carefully unpacked Old Faithful. It was the easiest camera to set up, so it would be the first camera in the water. The yellow cylinders were lifted out of their cases, and the camera loaded with a fresh film cassette containing enough film for 2,000 pictures. The cylinders were strapped to the frame, and the apparatus stood outside the garage to await transportation down to Temple Pier.

The garage was cluttered with the leftover equipment from previous expeditions. In one corner was the camera frame that had been dragged over the loch floor in 1974, and lying on the floor was the frame that had held Old Faithful in previous years. Countless other pieces of malfunctioning or discarded electronic equipment awaited rebirth by new hands. Dusty flyspecked windows looked out over the loch; and working in the garage, we found it difficult not to squint through the dust to look for a hump moving across the surface.

Next to the garage was the stone cottage in which Rines and his family were staying. It was the kind of cozy cottage, with lush rose bushes framing it, that teen-aged girls dream about settling down in with fantasized Prince Charmings. Attached to the cottage was a large stone storage barn that Rines was having converted into additional living area—downstairs a bedroom for his baby son Justice, and upstairs an observatory, where telescopes and cameras could be trained on the loch far below.

Rines had become so dedicated to his search for the beast that he had bought the cottage perched on the mountain to give him a base of operations and to allow a closer friendship with the local residents. One day while gazing across the loch from the opposite shore, he had pointed at the white speck of the cottage and declared to his wife, "I want to buy a house *there!*" So when the owner, Gordon Mac-Kintosh, had offered it to him, he had jumped at the chance. Since then, he and MacKintosh, who owns a sprawling, handsome house next door, had become good friends, and MacKintosh had proved an invaluable local ally in Rines' quest.

Work on the equipment continued into the afternoon, when Rines and Charlie first went down to the loch to string electrical cable for Old Faithful. Temple Pier was a cluster of buildings on the shore below the highway along the loch. There were the neat new houses of the Menzies family who owned the pier, and several decaying boat-houses. A stone jetty jutted about 100 feet out into the bay, and behind it was the new portable cottage that was to be used as a command post. Surprisingly, only about 200 feet offshore was the buoy marking the mooring from which the camera platforms were to be anchored. The loch bottom dropped sharply to about a 70-foot depth in this short distance, so the mooring was in quite deep water.

Charlie and Rines rowed out onto the cold tea-colored water and ran a black cable from the buoy at the mooring and up to one of the Menzies houses. Meanwhile Doc, McGowan, Wilford, and Jeffrey Thomason, a zoology student from Cambridge University, began the first sonar probe of the loch. They wanted to study the bottom sediments and measure the depths around the pier with Doc's old "bottom pinger," a sonar machine which shot a sonar beam straight down through the water and into the bottom. The expedition's activity at the loch had begun, and the usually quiet bay had experienced the last quiet moments it was to have for some time.

The unpacking, setting up of equipment, and rigging took all day, and not until late that evening did the first camera splash into the loch. Rines and Wyckoff rowed a rubber dinghy out of the mooring and I followed in a rowboat, holding Old Faithful's frame in place across the gunwales. Thomason manned the oars of the substantial rowboat, and Paul Hosefros, *The New York Times* photographer recorded the events on film. As we rowed out, a cold wind blew up, whipping the loch into waves. Perhaps I was being overdramatic, but I couldn't avoid feeling that somehow the loch protected the animal, and the rocking of the boats in the sudden wind was only one more portent. The camera was attached to the power line of the buoy, and its switch activated. The dependable strobe began flashing periodically; the familiar click-wheeze sound of the camera was reassuring. We maneuvered the frame clumsily onto the rubber boat, which was to act as the float for the camera. Later, the cabin cruiser *Hunter* would be brought down from Rines' cottage to support the camera gear. After checking the functioning of the light and camera, Rines and Wyckoff slipped the rig over the side, payed out the yellow nylon rope, and the camera sank abruptly from sight. The line was looped over the dinghy and secured, and Rines and Wyckoff climbed into the boat with us. Peering into the water, I made out a muted yellow flash from 20 feet below. Each darkened flash brought home powerfully the profound darkness that surrounded Old Faithful under the water. The elapsed-time camera had been set to take a picture every 15 seconds, so the film had to be changed every eight hours or so. Charlie was optimistic; if the creature were really attracted to the camera or the strobe, only a few film loads would be needed to prove it.

We rowed to shore, leaving the rubber dinghy floating alone on the loch. The light was dying, and the castle in the background looked brooding. It was a fairy-tale place; it was a fairy-tale adventure. Was the animal merely a fairy tale for easily excitable adults? Maybe one of the 2,000 pictures taken that night would assure us of the beast's reality. The camera had returned to its place in the bay; perhaps its visitor would, too.

Of course, Doc had come up with his own theory of why the beast was attracted to the camera, and he gleefully explained it to anyone who would listen:

"Now, here you've got this big animal, and he lives in a big lake with nothing but muck on the bottom, and no good rocks. So what does he do when he has an itch? There's nothing for him to scratch on.

"He's swimming along and he comes to these big metal cameras with lots of sharp corners, so he sort of sidles up to them and gets himself a good scratching, and we take his picture."

Doc would explain, with an impish grin, that Rines had gotten the 1972 pictures of the flipper because the beast was up close getting himself a good rub from the frame. Thus was born the "Edgerton Scratch Theory."

Early in the morning, on June 3, 1976, Charlie rowed out onto the loch to change Old Faithful's film. The camera was to be served faithfully by Charlie himself, who was a firm believer in the adage that begins "If you want something done right . . ."

We'd heard stories of the beast's huge hump emerging from the loch near boats and frightening the occupants out of their wits. Helping Charlie change the film in the elapsed-time camera that morning, I got an inkling of what the experience must have been like. As we pulled up the yellow camera, even Old Faithful, a familiar, friendly piece of apparatus, startled me when it suddenly heaved into view beneath the brown waters. I could almost visualize the jarring sight of a huge hump erupting to the surface, water streaming off it, and the waves breaking over it, hinting at an even greater bulk below the waterline. The loch had created a dramatic stage for the beast.

As we changed the film, Doc and Rines had gone out in a small rowboat with Doc's bottom-pinger to do some sonar studies in the middle of the loch. We watched their progress across the loch in the boat, amazed at how tiny they looked. The loch was not the pond it appeared to be, but a vast sheet of water. The mountains on either side gave the loch a sense of enclosure that made it seem much smaller. Since one could view large areas of its surface from a convenient height, one assumed that little danger could come from being on the loch. It was a deadly assumption; those experienced in the ways of the loch recognized it as a dangerous place. A human plunged into the frigid waters could survive only an hour or so before succumbing to the cold. And the enormous depths of the loch offered no chance of a swimmer's clambering into a shallow area. Doc and Rines, seemingly unconcerned, inched across the loch taking sonar readings, their boat bobbing about the 700-foot-deep watery abyss.

All went well in their sonar patrols, and Doc discovered some interesting features in the bottom geology that he, McGowan and Thomason investigated the next day with his side-scan sonar. Out in the middle they trailed the yellow torpedo through the water and examined a portion of the bottom and sides. That night, gathered around the kitchen table at Gordon MacKintosh's they pored over the data. Doc had a word for the poring—"hatching." No scientist worth his salt examined his results just once, figured out what he had, and then set the data aside. The data had to be "hatched"—analyzed again and again, talked about, chewed over, left and returned to. Scientists have propagated a flattering myth about themselves in their writings in learned journals; that they coolly and perfectly gather their evidence on the first try, analyze it precisely the first time, and then publish. Doc had been in the business of science a long time. He had garnered all the honors he needed, and he did not need the myth to hide behind while he figured out what the hell was going on.

At the kitchen table he leaned back, his feet out, and examined the sonar charts with the familiar air of a housewife reading a soup-can label. He surmised, theorized, dreamed, concocted silly theories and sage theories. Rines was as always the advocate, intense, interested; Charlie the matter-of-fact gatherer-of-data.

Doc's sonar records showed that the sediments sloped up gradually from the bottom of the loch onto the sides, as if material from the sides had slid down into the loch. The evidence could be applied to the theory that the loch's almost vertical sides actually extended straight down, meeting in a V-formation far below and the flat bottom was a sort of false bottom created by the sides slumping into the loch over tens of thousands of years.

They sat drawing on napkins and peering at the smudges on the sonar trace. The light outside was just beginning to dim at eleven o'clock at night. Suddenly Rines leaped to his feet and ran to the window. He thought he had seen something in the loch. I followed, electrified, almost running over him. But it was nothing. Doc and Charlie remained in their seats, forever cool. They would wait for Rines' confirmation; only then would they bother to see what was occurring on the loch. They knew that to figure out the mystery of the beast one couldn't go careering around, alternating between excitement and despair. That was the power of science; it rolled along unrelenting, steadily gathering all the data available, dispassionately throwing out what was undependable and romantic, but keeping that which was solid. Its practitioners would eventually take care of this Loch Ness mystery, opening up whole networks of new pathways for science to explore.

Rines stepped outside into the cool air, and we watched the darkening loch, the play of dying light over the surface and the mists just beginning to touch the air. The wind eased around the mountaintop, ruffling hair and chilling skin, and he was at once the romantic, remembering the electrifying effect of his monster sighting in 1971.

He dearly wanted his friends Doc and Charlie to "have a sighting." It would surely affect them the same way it had affected him, Tim Dinsdale, and the countless other people who had glimpsed a powerful hump rippling across the loch. The experience would fascinate, mesmerize; they would want to come back again and again, wanting to see more, to know more about the beast. It would become an obsession.

Rines wanted Doc and Charlie to become fascinated with the search because they were his friends, but also because he badly needed them and the other technologists. They alone had the technological power to make his hunt work. Their fingers sparked with it as they thumbed through the sonar records or assembled the cameras. They could shape a flow of electrons, focus rays of light, pull images onto film for him. Each had control over a particular corner of the physical universe, and Rines needed all of them to wrest information from those corners for him to fling at the world.

He wanted the world to understand the value of human testimony to science. Scientists had disregarded the beast in the past because it had been witnessed by "mere" humans, rather than their precious instruments. To elevate humans to their proper place as sources of scientific evidence, Rines had to prove the existence of the beast on science's terms, even if it meant changing his style to match the cool, unemotional mien of science. Before his successes, his reports of expeditions had been full of exclamation points, leading questions, innuendo, excited verbiage. But things had changed with the new expedition. No longer did he write that he wanted to "solve the mystery of the Loch Ness monster." Now, it was "obtain further evidence relating to the aquatic animals at Loch Ness."

If he gave science the kind of evidence it understood—photographs, sonar traces, and bones—maybe then science would realize its neglect of the human evidence of sightings. It might begin to heed other kinds of human evidence, not accepted before because it couldn't be revealed in terms of decimal points and orders of magnitude.

Knowing Rines the clever joker, his old friends believed that his Loch Ness evidence had been a huge prank, and it was, in a sophisticated, reverse-twist sort of way—for his evidence was legitimate! Rines would really prove that this magical beast existed, and he would sweep science into a fun-house world where witches and warlocks, ghosts and leprechauns, and all sorts of other wondrous creatures were possible. Science would find itself in front of one of those hilariously distorted mirrors. In the distortion, it would perhaps see itself in a clearer, saner, more mature way than ever before.

Rines would force science to confront the fact that it was, in the end, just a more successful form of magic. It was as dependent as magic on human perception and subjectivity, and it was as passive as magic, relying for its discoveries strictly on the phenomena Nature allowed it to witness.

This assault on science was a nasty thing for Rines to do; science had cherished the notion that it was superior to human subjectivity; that it alone listened to nature. Here was Rines claiming that nature talked to everybody; the witch doctors of science were to learn that others had their magic too, and it was just as good as science's.

There was no doubt he would have the world's attention, as the melee surrounding the next day's installation of the TV/stereo frame would show. *The New York Times,* in the person of Wilford and Hosefros, was there to report the first lowering of the system. NBC had hired a British film crew and assorted consultants to record the action for its television special. The 16-foot research boat *Hunter* had been moved down from Rines' cottage and moored off Temple Pier, and was ready to act as the float for suspending the camera frames.

Old Faithful was ferried out to the *Hunter* first, in a large wooden boat, shepherded by Rines and Wyckoff. It was a rough, blustery day, and even in the shelter of Urquhart Bay, the boats and men were blown about fiercely. The clouds whipped across the sky, and their shadows formed a moving, dappling pattern across the valley. Charlie was in especially bad straits; the pressures of the expedition had apparently lowered his resistance, and he had contacted a vicious virus. But, bundled up, and with a Sherlock Holmes deerstalker cap pulled down around his ears, he was determined to be there. ("If you want something done right. . . .")

On the *Hunter,* Rines and Charlie hoisted Old Faithful up onto the bow overlooking the brown waves. On shore, I was given a signal and flipped the power switch activating the power from the shore to the boat. A delightful blast of light answered from Old Faithful's strobe, aimed at me from the *Hunter.* Satisfied that everything was working, the engineers edged the camera frame over the side and into the water, suspending it from the bow of the *Hunter,* which bucked wildly under the impact of the waves. The 250-pound TV/stereo rig was then slid off the pier and onto the rowboat. As the rowboat fought its way out to the *Hunter,* we payed out the black cable which ran up to the control cabin. The little boats on the wind-whipped loch rose and fell in unison as the camera rig was wrestled onto the *Hunter.*

A local resident—a mountain of a fellow named Tony Gerling—manhandled the frame up onto the boat. This was the big moment. *The New York Times* would herald the splashdown of the equipment triumphantly, but the press experienced some technical difficulties in obtaining the story. *The Times* photographer and the press officer—me—spent the splashdown period skewing wildly about in an absurd little dinghy tossed around on the loch like a twig. I fought the wind and the loch, and the boat as well. The oars kept jumping out of the oarlocks, one arm got more tired than the other, and I rowed in circles, looping round and round the *Hunter* with the people on board smirking as we flashed by. It was only by chance that the rowboat lurched wildly past the *Hunter* as the main rig splashed into the water and sank from view. The moment was captured on film for posterity and for *The Times*.

The rig was 20 feet down in the silent depths of the loch, hanging from the side of the *Hunter*. There was still considerable adjusting to be done. With much ship-to-shore shouting, it had been established that nothing was yet visible on the television monitor in the control cottage. With paddles, boathooks, and whatever other implements were handy, the men in the boat jimmied the ropes supporting the cameras around to aim the television camera at Old Faithful. Handling and aiming the cameras would be improved considerably once the large research raft was constructed to support the cameras, but the *Hunter* would do well for now.

Finally came the glorious moment when the elapsed-time camera bobbed into view on the television screen. As the waves buffeted the *Hunter*, the boat yanked like a mad puppeteer on the lines supporting the two camera frames. Old Faithful bounced, twisted, and lurched wildly on and off the television screen. Occasionally the frame lurched downward so far we could see the strobe light which was five feet above the camera on the frame. Especially interesting was that, no matter how violent the buffeting, the camera steadfastly held its horizontal aim. Clearly no errant wave had knocked the camera upward in the 1975 film.

The television picture was quite dim deep under the loch, even with a powerful light on the TV/stereo rig trained on Old Faithful. The gleaming surface of the gyrating camera left a luminous, ghostly train on the dim television screen as it bobbed about. The camera and strobe assembly looked to us like a tempting bait, jiggling about and flashing 20 feet beneath the boat. If the beast took this lovely piece of bait as it had last year, we would be ready, and someone on our team might just be the first human to see the Loch Ness monster in its natural habitat.

Unexpected problems appeared in the completed camera assemblage that hadn't shown up in the individual parts. For instance, periodically the bait camera would twist around, aiming toward the television camera, and its strobe light would loose a brilliant flash toward the TV/stereo rig. This flash would trigger the slave strobe light on the

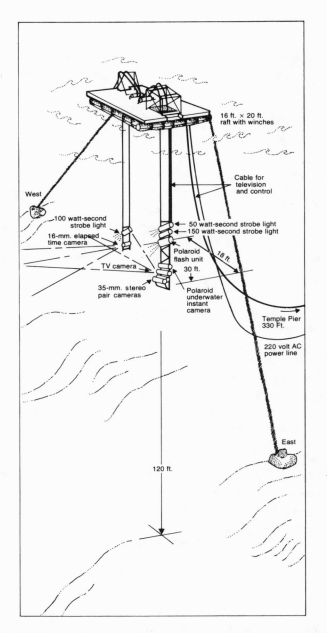

The 1976 expedition used two separate camera frames, hanging
in the loch. On one frame was Old Faithful, the 16–mm. elapsed-
time camera, which was to act as the bait. On the other frame,
aimed at Old Faithful were the TV, stereo, and Polaroid cameras.
(*Alumni Association of M.I.T.*)

big rig, which would answer the little camera with its own blast of light. The two camera rigs had developed a relationship—one enticing the other into draining the battery energy in its strobe light. Nobody could have predicted such equipment idiosyncrasies, much less the myriad of natural phenomena that had frustrated monsterhunters in the past.

The tiny glassed-in porch that was the monitoring room in the control cottage held a welter of tools, cameras, electronic parts, and, of course, the monitoring system. Crowded onto a small table were the videotape recorder, the two television monitors, the control box, and a spaghettilike confusion of wires connecting them. Snaking wildly under the table and around the edge of the floor was a string of apparata designed to change the 220-volt, 50-cycle British current into 110-volt, 60-cycle American. This metamorphosis was needed because the television tape had to be the standard American kind to be useful in America. It would be the ultimate irony, said the monster-hunters, to obtain a mind-blowing videotape of the beast attacking the cameras, and not be able to show it in America.

The circuitry for changing the current was one of Doc's amazing Rube Goldberg contraptions; and we believed he kept it functioning purely by dint of his mystical personal powers over electronic equipment. The apparatus was a "kneebone-connected-to-the-thighbone" array.

The electrical outlet in the cottage was connected to the power inverter; the inverter was connected to the transformer; the transformer was connected to the battery charger; the battery charger was connected to the batteries, and (whew!) finally, the batteries were connected to the videotape recorder. Only a wizard like Doc could have fiddled together such a wild array.

After careful adjustments of the electronic equipment, the underwater cameras were ready to go. The only operation left was to trigger the stereo cameras several times to advance unexposed film into place in the camera. In a happy little ceremony, the white stereo button was pressed three times—by Esther Edgerton, Helen Wyckoff, and Joni Meredith. Now we were ready for the animal.

At 6:45 P.M., on June 6, 1976, I took the first watch on the underwater cameras as the others went off to rest and dine. After the whirl of activity of that day, it was an eerie contrast, being left so totally alone to stare at the ghostly image of the elapsed-time camera on the television screen. A sudden jerk of the camera on the screen would send me lurching forward to place my fingers on the white buttons of the control box. I could almost feel the camera's bouncing in the pit of my stomach. None of us had the slightest idea what the animal would look like on the screen. Would the camera merely disappear from the screen? Would a dark blot obscure everything? Or would there appear a hideous head, a powerful flipper? Doc gave me the full benefit of his years of underwater photography, as he left, delivering a very short lecture on monster-photography.

"Don't be bashful," he said.

I was well primed emotionally for my watch, for there were hints that the animals were already in the vicinity. Word had come from Rines that people living near Temple Pier, looking out over the water a couple of evenings before, had seen the light from the submerged Old Faithful skewing about wildly underwater, sending its light streaming to the surface like a beam from hell. Thus, Charlie believed the expedition was very likely already a success and that we probably had photographs of the beast from the elapsed-time camera.

So, I sat there, my eyes never leaving the screen, ultraconscious of the long black cable running from my television out a nearby window, down to the pier, into the water, across the loch bottom, and into a camera that could show me a creature which had scared grown men out of their wits.

Doc predicted that people would quickly become bored with staring at the screen, and I did lapse into reveries. But my reflexes were set on hair-trigger. The slightest wrong move by the bait camera, the smallest suspicious twist or turn or bob, and I would jump forward from my chair, my heart thumping reaching for the white buttons to fire the cameras.

My first watch, however, came to a rather ignominious end. As I sat hypnotized by the bouncing, weaving camera, I became aware that something was changing about the equipment. The whine of the electronics had altered pitch, almost imperceptibly. The television picture was growing smaller. "No, it couldn't be; just my imagination," I thought. But slowly, the whole system gave up the electronic ghost, the television picture shrinking to nothing. Without Doc's magic to keep the charging system going, it had pooped out. It was unable to keep up with the electrical load of the television camera and videotape recorder.

I sat there for a while feeling quite foolish, watching a dark screen until Bob and Doc returned and shut the equipment off. They would resurrect it in the morning. It was an orderly retreat from the loch; they had achieved a major victory in just getting the camera down safely. Rines knew how easy it was to have the loch destroy months of work in a few moments. It was perhaps best not to push the loch too hard.

The next day, June 7, the expedition held a press conference at which Rines activated his lawyer-switch to convince a couple of dozen reporters that we were serious honest folk out on a serious scientific adventure. The reporters dutifully took notes and journeyed down to lochside to view the equipment. The television crews were content to interview Rines, film Charlie pulling up Old Faithful and, most amusing, to film each other filming Rines (who was installing film in the camera to film the beast). The expedition was a marketable media commodity, as *The New York Times* had discovered. It had sold newspaper rights to the story around the world and, of course, NBC proposed to elevate the expedition to video-legend with its television special. The NBC film team had hired a caravan of cars and trucks and turned the little pier and the tiny control hut into an active film set. We were constantly asked to pretend to watch the television scenes, to stage meetings, and to play-act for the cameras. I began to realize the irony of the phrase "true-life adventure," so often used to describe documentaries. The television filming was fun, but added another Alice-in-Wonderland factor to the already dreamlike expedition. Imagine, not only were we on this crazy adventure in a fairy-tale loch to film a beast many considered a joke, but we had to reenact everything for the cameras.

The reporters and television crews had departed by early afternoon, and Doc had coaxed the electrical circuits back into operation. Once more I took a watch. Again, I relaxed in the lawn chair on the glassed-in porch; again there was the bobbing, weaving camera; and again it would abruptly zip off the screen, scaring the devil out of me. If the cameras' tricks weren't bad enough, there was a capricious breeze blowing through the hut. I would be watching the screen quietly, my nerves on edge, and suddenly a newspaper on the floor would flap in the breeze, startling me out of my chair. The long hours, the frustration and the mini-coronaries were all well worth it. The television was showing a potentially more exciting program than any of the shoot-

'em-ups on broadcast television. If something exciting showed on my screen, it would be the real thing.

Each watch had its own character, and this watch was a relaxed one. It was one of those beautiful sunny days the loch served up rather stingily. A mild wind played across the loch, producing gentle waves. In the distance, through the window, I could see British army troops training on the loch in kayaks. I got into the rhythm of the steady bobbing of the camera. I could feel the waves. I almost became the camera, flashing out into the water, easily snapping pictures of the cool, swimming peat particles. Monster? There was no monster in the peaceful loch. Absurd.

At the press conference that day, Doc had stressed how much superior our equipment was this year; we were putting the human into the control loop. No more click-wreezing away blindly into the loch as Rines had done in the past. I, the human, would be there, not only to get a picture, but to get a good picture. I could wait, watch, recognize, interpret, understand. I was firmly in the loop ready to actuate if something approached and I saw it on the screen—eyeball to optic nerve to occipital lobe to frontal lobe to all those little finger muscles: Pow! I would press the white buttons to take *the* pictures. But nothing happened on this watch either, and after a few hours of lazy monitoring—whistling and singing to fill the silence of the television picture —I was relieved.

That afternoon I arrived back to find Doc on watch. The loch had subsided to a dead calm; it was what veteran monster-hunters call a "Nessie day," because the beast is most often seen on the surface then. The elapsed-time camera hung leadenly in front of the television camera. The whine of the power inverter and the tape recorder seemed to collect in the room. Problems had arisen. The strobe lights on the TV/stereo rig were not working for some reason. When the white buttons were pushed, no flash was seen on the television screen. And electrical interference had made the videotape recorder practically useless at slow time-lapse speed. When something was recorded at the slow speed and played back, the picture was ripped apart by interference from the British current. Again, we put off full 24-hour watches until tomorrow, when we could pull the big unit up and check it.

The next day, June 8, 1976, brought the excitement of what we thought to be our first sighting of the beast. The evidence was subtle, subject to debate and discussion. For such vague evidence the fairest way was to give a percentage that the animal had been sighted, as a weatherman gives a percentage of the chance of rain. In this case, it might have been "65 percent chance of beast."

McGowan and Thomason had been out in the *Malaran*, a 33-foot cabin cruiser rented for the sonar search. They were chugging down the loch enjoying the sun when, peering out across the water, they saw a large wake coursing across the loch. Theirs was the only boat in sight, so they were certain the wake wasn't caused by another boat. But perhaps it was their own wake. They sped up the *Malaran*, tearing down the loch to create as large a wake as possible, then turned to see the damage they had done to the smooth loch surface. "Our wake was minuscule compared to the wake we had seen," said McGowan. Thomason said he got the impression of blobs of some sort in the midst of the wake, and when Carol Rines produced a copy of the picture of a large wake she had taken in 1975, with blobs in the middle, he said that was much like what he saw. Had Thomason seen the horns of the creature coursing across the loch?

Doc and Charlie paid the nebulous report little mind, but the NBC film crew leaped on it, interviewing McGowan and Thomason for all they were worth. But no matter how inconsequential, the sighting still put an edge on the day, as did the final successful adjustments on the TV/stereo rig. After hoisting the rig aboard the *Hunter*, Rines, Doc and Charlie found that water had leaked into the largest strobe. Doc brought it back to shore for repairs, while the others checked out the Polaroid, which apparently suffered from a faulty electrical contact.

We discovered that the loch had punished the equipment even more severely than we'd thought and the frame for the TV/stereo camera had to be beefed up to withstand the strain. Also, the ropes and suspension were rearranged to aim more stably at Old Faithful. But these were all expected adjustments, made with willing hands, and even delight. The engineers actually seemed to want a few things to go wrong, so they could fiddle with the gear, a fun prospect for technologists. By early in the evening, Doc had fixed the strobe cylinder and carried it back out to the *Hunter*. He had sauntered back into the control hut trilling "It's spring, trala, trala!" a happy man. After the repairs, the crew sent the camera rig over the edge of the boat with a heave, and slid it gently back into the loch. On shore we watched the ghostly image of Old Faithful come back into view. I settled down at 7:15 for another uneventful watch.

The next morning Charlie boarded a plane for London, to find a film laboratory to develop the growing pile of film from the elapsed-time camera. There was little use in click-wheezing away with Old Faithful until we knew we were getting good pictures, so we decided to wait until Charlie returned with the processed film to resume watching. Late that night he did, and I was awakened at midnight by an excited, conspiratorial Rines gliding into my hotel room in the darkness. "Things are looking good!" he whispered. His eyes almost glowed in the dark. "Charlie's back and he's looked at the elapsed-time film. It looks good, and we're going to monitor all night tonight." His excitement was catching. I found myself awaking with a start three hours later to drive along the dark road to the pier for an uneventful 3:00 A.M.-to-6:00 A.M. watch. Joni and I were by no means discouraged, and we decided to camp overnight in the hut to watch all the next night.

We began our all-night vigil the next evening, June 10, 1976, at 8:00 P.M. As we settled into the hut, we knew Rines and Charlie were on an even more exciting mission. That day Rines told me of a report "from an individual who knows his animals," that the person had seen a dark four-foot-long animal he couldn't identify, move sinuously across the road in front of his car a few nights before. Rines was as excited as a schoolboy; Charlie was matter-of-fact, but a certain twinkle in the eye betrayed him. They were both full of theories and speculation. The beast had been seen several times on land in the past. Despite the heavily traveled highway beside the loch, its shoreline was not well explored. There were narrow beaches so hidden by underbrush that they were visible from neither the road nor the loch. Who knew what could lurk there?

The night before, Rines and Charlie had explored up and down the narrow rocky shore, poking into bushes and crawling under rock faces. Charlie had found a bone that McGowan would be asked to examine. And he had discovered a hidden culvert crossing under the road, through which could pass a . . . who-knew-what?

But all was to be kept secret—they didn't want it known that one of the beasts might be available for capture. Neither did they want to look foolish. They were public figures now, not just scientists, and with the intense publicity surrounding the expedition they had lost that cherished right of any scientist—to tear off on wild-goose-chases.

I daydreamed about what they could find as I went off to bed leaving Joni to the first watch. My daughter Wendy had finished her usual busy day of poking into every corner of the research site and keeping an eye on "Uncle Doc." She went peacefully off to sleep in one of the cottage's bedrooms. She had adjusted well to being shunted to a different continent, a different time zone, and a succession of strange beds. The eerie atmosphere of the loch at night had gotten to Joni; she locked all the doors in the cottage before wrapping herself tightly in a blanket and settling down in the dark room to stare at the glowing television screen. Marriage means adjusting to some odd situations, but I'm sure when we took our marriage vows Joni never thought she would end up sitting beside a loch in Scotland watching all night for the Loch Ness monster to stick his head in front of a television camera.

At 12:45 A.M. I took over. That night was among my most vivid memories of the loch, not because of the beast, but because of the overwhelming beautiful mood of the loch. All was dead still. The bait camera hung peacefully in front of the television camera. It was the kind of sleepy fishing—with a technological lure—that every fisherman enjoys, even if he doesn't catch anything. Just me and Old Faithful—I watched it, and it watched the silent loch.

I stepped outside to escape the humming electronics, and was greeted with a massive quiet. The *Hunter* sat unmoving on the water easily visible in the semidarkness. The air was tickled only by the delicate calls of the night birds. I could see the dark form of the castle across the bay; and across the loch, the mountains loomed in silhouette against a sky just preparing to become light. It was magical; a loch so huge, so deep, yet so still.

I stepped back into the cottage which was full of the whine and warmth from the electronics. The litter was homey. Cluttering the floor were wires, tools, and electronic parts, and the incredible, intertwined mishmash of Doc's magic monster machine. The small television monitors on the table sat upon one another, perched on an overturned trash can. They had been supported by a cardboard box which threatened to collapse at any moment, so the instrument platform was duly replaced. I periodically retreated from one environment into the other—from the magnificent primitive loch to the man-made environment of the electronified cottage. It was a profound contrast, going backward in time to the ancient loch, and forward to the world of transistors and television.

As the sky became lighter, the birds began to test their songs for the day. I could hear the distant sounds of cuckoos and geese and the chirp of songbirds. It grew lighter, and a shaft of sunlight struck the castle tower. The trees on the opposite shore, two miles away also became visible. So incredibly clear was the air, and so low the angle of light, that each tree stood out starkly, as if it were the only one on the mountain, trying its best to be a forest.

Soon Joni woke up, other expedition members began arriving, and my experience alone with the loch was over. I quite understood then why Tim Dinsdale had given up a career and would leave his beloved family for months at a time to drift alone and lonely on the loch. It was the home of a fabulous beast, but it was also a place where nature spoke profoundly.

That day Charlie Finkelstein arrived to begin the sonar search, and at a meeting that night we crowded into the tiny living room of the cottage to hear the sonar team's plans. McGowan said he had to assume that the animals died randomly throughout the loch, so the searchers had an equal chance everywhere on the loch of finding a carcass. However, a carcass could more easily be recovered in the shallow areas—a diver could reach it—so the sonar scans would be concentrated there.

Rines thought the searchers should heed some of the loch's legends, which said that the beast lurked around the ruined Urquhart Castle. He waned Finkelstein and McGowan to search there, especially around an odd underwater peak that jutted up sharply near the castle. Perhaps a dead beast would become lodged at the base of the peak.

Finkelstein would certainly have excellent equipment for detecting objects on the bottom. Arriving soon from the United States would be Klein's prototype sonar system which could scan both the loch bottom on either side of the side-scan fish and probe bottom sediments with a third sonar beam aimed straight down.

Before any serious scanning could get underway, though, Finkelstein had to learn much more about the loch. Seeing with sonar was like seeing with the eye. One first had to orient oneself; learn to focus on the important part of the scene; discover the tricks the environment could play on the vision. It required an almost instinctive feel for the waters and loch bottom passing beneath the towed sonar fish. Finkelstein would have to understand the effect of layers of differing temperatures under the loch, of the chemical makeup of the water, of the objects and sediment patterns on the bottom, and of countless other unforeseeable factors.

The sonar team also had to lay out navigation markers on the shore, to triangulate where the boat was at all times; for no matter how sensational their discovery, it would be useless if they couldn't navigate their way back to it later. They might have to take the sonar records back to shore, even back to the United States, and do some data-hatching before they would really know what the sonar had revealed.

Like Doc and the others, Finkelstein also favored installing a sonar beam to watch the underwater cameras. As it was, we had no idea what was approaching the cameras. We might already have been unknowingly visited. The beast could have hovered just out of camera range, and we would have had no inkling of its presence.

At the meeting that evening, we heard the disappointing news that the mysterious sinuous object moving across the road a few nights back had been a huge black cat. Rines and Charlie had discovered the animal in their forays. And the bone Charlie found was probably a cow's, McGowan had said. Another exciting possibility shattered, but hope sprang eternal.

The monitoring continued for another week, and we got to know the bounces and twists of the elapsed-time camera very well. Doc, Rines and Charlie began to believe that something about the apparatus repelled the beast. Maybe it was the bewildering tangle of equipment and cables strung beneath the loch, or perhaps it was the steady lights trained on Old Faithful to keep it visible to the television camera. They tried leaving the steady lights off, but the ploy seemed not to work.

Our sense of claustrophobia toward the television mounted. The television camera could see so little. What was going on behind it, around it? Were we attracting anything to the general vicinity of the cameras? Charlie's experience on one early-morning tour of duty made the watchers even more certain that they needed a sonar beam monitoring the area. Around midnight on June 16, 1976, as Charlie watched the television screen, he noticed that the elapsed-time camera was fading from view—as if silt were flowing between it and the television camera. Charlie pressed the buttons triggering the stereo cameras, but there was so much murk that no flash could be seen on the television screen. It was an odd set of circumstances, for there were no boats, currents, or wind to stir up sediment. Was something near the cameras agitating the bottom? Charlie peered out the door of the control hut and saw that the *Hunter* was pointing toward the pier. But all the other boats moored in the area were pointing at a right angle, toward the mouth of the bay.

Charlie pressed the button again and could barely see the other camera in the flash from the powerful strobes. Four minutes later, the elapsed-time camera seemed to move off the screen violently to the right. Charlie pressed the button again, and another powerful surge of light shot through the water. But there was nothing there, not even the camera.

About one o'clock in the morning, the elapsed-time camera floated back into sight. The waters gradually cleared. The episode was over, leaving Charlie mystified. He had no idea whether he had encountered the creature. He was exhausted and went to bed. It had been a harrowing night.

News of Charlie's encounter produced an air of excitement, at the meeting the next evening. A new contingent of the expedition had arrived and a new round of plans had to be made. John Lothrop had brought an improved Polaroid SX–70 underwater camera that could neatly fit onto the camera frame to replace the old one. He had taken the time between the first wave of expedition members and his departure for the loch to build a unit that would be easier to load and could take better pictures with less light. The experienced Lothrop had many tricks up his photographic sleeve; he had even brought along a supply of experimental Polaroid film, should the SX–70 need still more sensitivity. Lothrop would also remedy the expedition's lack of mobility by salvaging broken underwater cameras from previous expeditions to build a portable camera-strobe system.

He set to work on his projects the next morning. A quiet, friendly man, he had worked for Polaroid for decades, doing what he loved most—building cameras. So what better vacation than to fly across the ocean to a beautiful Scottish loch . . . and build cameras? He and Charlie worked with each other as if they had been lifelong friends— two gentlemen cameramen off on a spree. They scrounged scrap boards to build a float to test out the silhouette camera. They reloaded Old

Faithful, tinkered about on miscellaneous projects, and generally had a grand time.

Slowly but surely, under Lothrop's steady workmanlike care, the new camera system grew. He repaired one of the underwater cameras from the 1975 sonar-triggered system, adjusted its innards to take pictures once every 15 seconds, and built an aluminum frame from scraps of the old rig. He made the case from another underwater camera into a battery case, attaching it to the frame to make the unit totally self-contained. The system was completed by a strobe light mounted at the top of the frame, and the expedition became a portable monster-hunting safari!

A new direction for the search was badly needed. After two weeks of waiting for the beast, the expedition had lapsed into ennui. Watching was more casual, and there was little feeling of expectation.

The slowing down was not just a result of frustration; Doc, Charlie, and Rines had been on enough expeditions to know that one didn't work one's scientific head off unless there was reason to expect some results. An easy rhythm of effort had to be established for a long-term effort. Doc declared that it had taken five years of work to get lousy pictures, and we should be prepared to spend another five years to get good ones.

The latest theory on why one of the animals hadn't shown itself was that the migrating salmon had not yet come into the loch from the North Sea. There was talk that the droughts in the area had lowered the level of the Ness River so much that the fish couldn't get into the loch. Others were fearful that the fish had been severely depleted by over-fishing in the Atlantic.

Like all other scientists, the monster-hunters were ready to theorize at the drop of a very small hat, even batting around ideas about a beast they'd never seen and perhaps never would. Building theories, even on practically nonexistent evidence, was actually a very pleasant, harmless diversion; it gave the theorizers something to do, made them feel that they were dynamically on the trail of the mystery, and a theory could even turn out to be right!

On June 17, 1976, a nervous Charlie Finkelstein finally got a chance to dive in the loch to inspect the cameras and pose for them as a stand-in "monster." As he donned his black wetsuit, splashed into the loch, and appeared on the television screen, we came to truly understand how he could be nervous about being underwater with the beast. Finkelstein was such a large dark shape in his black wetsuit, that the animal might easily mistake him for another Nessie. What if it were mating season! What a prospect to be approached by a lovesick 30-foot underwater creature!

Finkelstein surfaced from his dive with good news and bad news. The good news was that he could see much better than he had thought below the surface, and all he needed was a good light to explore the loch. The bad news was that the heavy TV/stereo rig was not as sturdy as it should have been. The steady bouncing appeared to be loosening the top crossbar, and we had visions of the expensive cameras plunging to the bottom and into the silt.

While underwater examining the cameras, Finkelstein had tried to imagine what the beast would think upon seeing the cameras. He said he was now convinced that no large animal in its right mind would approach the flashing, shiny mass of cameras with the tangle of wires and mooring lines. The equipment had to be simplified, neatened up, made more presentable to any underwater eyes which might be watching. Finkelstein also had more disturbing thoughts while floating in the darkness of the loch.

"The only apprehension you have about diving in Loch Ness is good old Nessie. You try to place yourself on the outside looking in, and you see yourself sitting there with your little light playing it around; and Nessie could be just over there and you wouldn't know it."

Finkelstein was an experienced enough diver to know that, whether a beast lived in the loch or not, the fear of one could make a diver nervous; cause him to make mistakes—kill him. Finkelstein wanted a safe ring of bright lights around him if he was to work underwater in the loch. The lights certainly wouldn't make any difference if a two-ton animal decided to rush out of the darkness after him, but it would make him feel better. It was a nightlight to ward off bogeymen, but they were psychological bogeymen that could mean a quick death.

Finkelstein also noticed strange buoyancy problems while diving. After carefully adjusting his weights for neutral buoyancy, he would be floating serenely in midwater, when suddenly he would find himself moving upward or downward. Many others who had gone underwater in the loch had similarly concluded it was a peculiar place. There might be freak currents and eddies, perhaps due to cracks or fissures in the bottom. In 1969 an 11-ton submarine had been exploring deep in the loch when it was suddenly swirled around by a strange vortex as if it were a toy. The submarine had blown all its ballast to surface and escaped the vortex.

Another remarkable feature noticed by Finkelstein in his dive was the steep dropoff of the loch bottom. The camera equipment overlooked an underwater ledge which plummeted over 200 feet down in distance of a few hundred feet. The steep sides of the mountains around the shore continued just as steeply under the loch.

That evening the sonar team and some joy-riders went out for the first test run with the sonar towfish. It was a clear, cool Scottish dusk, with the sun already set, but still diffusing its light evenly over the sky. We cast off from the pier, and the *Malaran* moved out into the loch with a low rumble from its motors. Watching the large wake, we concluded that the beast must be a remarkable animal if it left a wake twice as large as that of this 33-foot cabin cruiser. We first took a quick jaunt around the area of the Urquhart Castle, a "monster run" to see if anything interesting was on the surface. Might as well make sure. The castle looked small from across the bay, but up close it had all the magnificence that a medieval castle required to maintain its reputation. The crumbling walls jutted up from smooth, well-kept lawns on a bluff 40 feet above the loch surface. The tower of rough stone, with two of its walls missing, rose another 65 feet.

We saw nothing surfacing around the castle, so the *Malaran* made its way down the loch for the first test of the side-scan sonar. The heavy yellow cable was clipped onto the four-foot yellow towfish, and the switch activated. The sonar pulses were loud clicks spewing from the sides of the fish resting on the deck. The equipment appeared to be in good working order after shipment from the United States. With the boat barely moving, the fish was lifted over the stern, and lowered gently into the water, disappearing immediately. The cable was played out around an old automobile wheel rim attached to the *Malaran*'s mast. The boat moved out down the loch, and the cable tautened, vibrating slightly as the fish followed underwater. It was nearing midnight, and darkness was at last descending over the loch. The few shore lights showing indicated how sparsely the loch was settled, perhaps helping explain why there had been so few sightings of the beast. We towed the fish on a course parallel to the shore, about

200 yards out, watching the recorder printout for the undercuts and ridges in the side that Klein had found in 1970. Local tales had it that these caves were where the beasts hid.

There was much more to gathering good data with the sonar fish than merely throwing it overboard and trolling. The boat had to be piloted just so, to keep the towfish at the proper depth and on a straight course. Turns had to be executed smoothly and in a wide arc, so the expensive fish would not be damaged by the boat's propeller.

We inched down the loch, with Finkelstein in the cabin hovering over the recorder, which slowly reeled out paper with brown dapples indicating return echoes from the bottom.

The right side of the fish was seeing well. The sonar pulses bounced off the steep underwater slope of the shore and gave good pattern on the paper record. But the other side of the fish saw nothing, for it was pulsing out into the 700-foot depths of the loch and encountering only open water.

Finkelstein operated the machine as if communing with the electronic spirits within it, sensing the best settings. He knew his electronics well; so well that he had little trust for anything electronic. He declared that he allowed nothing that his life really depended on to contain electronics. He understood how a faulty connection or a transistor that didn't feel quite right that day could obliterate a whole circuit. His insurance against fickle electronics was an attaché case crammed with dozens of neatly arranged repair tools and a separate box with a multitude of spare electronic parts, carefully arranged in little unfolding partitions. Whereas Doc relied on his ability to fiddle things into shape. Finkelstein worked his magic more by the book. It was not as exciting, but it was far safer.

Finkelstein's lack of faith in electronics was rewarded that night on the loch; the sonar had been jostled in transit to the loch, and thin brown slashes were appearing across the paper showing that the system was acting up. He would have to spend a great deal of time alone with the sonar to discover what was wrong and repair it. We headed back into shore, homing on the lone light shining out from the control cottage. After some careful turning and backing, the *Malaran* edged gently up to the stone pier. The sonar search would go well.

In every human effort there seems to be a period when all the gremlins that have infested the adventure unite into a nasty mob. June 19 and 20, 1976, was that period for the Loch Ness expedition. A string of connected problems beset Finkelstein. He couldn't really fix the sonar unless he towed the sonar fish; to do this he had to remove the heavy bottom-penetrating sonar attachment on the front of the fish, and tow the fish alone; to do this he had to add more lead weights to the nose of the fish to give it the proper balance; to do this he had to call Martin Klein in the United States to find out how much weight to add; and to do this he had to deal with the British Tinkertoy telephone system.

There were problems with the underwater cameras, too. The power inverter, part of Doc's circuit to change from British to American current, had given out. Without it the videotape recorder could not run. But that didn't matter. Nothing could be seen on the monitor screen anyway because the transformer powering the lights illuminating Old Faithful had burned out, too.

Besides that, the batteries in the main underwater strobe light had run down, and in the confusion, hadn't been changed when the TV/stereo rig was hauled up to install the new Polaroid camera.

But even if the whole system had worked perfectly, there still appeared to be no beast for it to see. By now Charlie had examined 24,000 pictures from Old Faithful, which had been flashing away steadily at the rate of 2,000 pictures per day. He had seen nothing on the films but a few fish and the other camera, as Old Faithful occasionally twisted about to photograph the TV/stereo rig.

But there was still hope. The film cassette on which Old Faithful might have recorded Charlie's mysterious midnight episode with the silt in front of the TV was still in London being developed. Perhaps it would reveal what had gone on beneath the loch that night. There would be a short breathing spell before the adventurers began to use another method which could show that large moving objects were approaching the area of the cameras. A sonar, mounted on the bottom, would be the team's new eyes under the loch.

🏵 Chapter Five
THE LOCH

We had spent our time thus far at Loch Ness in a dogged, single-minded effort to capture the beast's image. It was a pure problem in optics and electronics: all we had to do was assemble the right combination of cameras to produce the right picture.

But we could never understand the beast, no matter how excellent our photographs, until we understood the glen and its people. In this cold, isolated land a complex web of relationships had been built up among the beast, the humans, and their home, the magnificent slash in the earth's crust known as the Great Glen of Scotland. Over the thousands of years, they had come to affect one another profoundly.

The expedition was a good experiment, and like any good experiment, it raised more questions than it answered. These questions raised more questions, which raised more, and so on, producing an avalanche of curiosity to be satisfied. So, as the expedition settled into a routine, curiosity pushed me to explore the Great Glen and its history.

Even from the beginning, the Great Glen was a peculiar place. It was only accidentally a part of the British Isles, originally attached to what is today Canada and Greenland—on the "wrong" side of the ancient proto-Atlantic Ocean. The Great Glen Fault, geologists believe, was born 350 million years ago as one section of a long crack in the earth stretching for hundreds of miles through Canada, along the present coast of Maine and Massachusetts, and ending in Rhode Island. The crack in the earth was born in the violence of the monumental collision between Europe and America, one' of the collisions that squeezed the ancient proto-Atlantic Ocean into nonexistence between the continents.

Some monster-hunters believe the beast in the loch is a remnant of the age of amphibians, when air-breathing creatures had just begun to crawl onto land. If so, the beast would have witnessed the birth of the Great Glen, for this period of prehistory was the amphibians' time to rule the earth. What poetic justice if the beast and the valley that would protect it were born at the same time!

The glen might have remained part of the North American continent had not the continents, in their ponderous collision, each torn off and kidnapped pieces of the other. In this exchange of land, Europe kidnapped northern Scotland, which contains the Great Glen. As the two continents inched apart, the Great Glen Fault left the rest of the fault behind in America. The land of the glen was no deep, cool haven then, but probably a deadly drought-stricken expanse of desert pavement and arroyos. The proto-Atlantic Ocean, which would have given moisture to the air, had disappeared in the collision between the continents.

But as the continents began to part again, 130 million years ago, a new moisture-giving Atlantic Ocean was formed, and the glen grew more hospitable. The dinosaurs that inhabited it then flourished. Some believe the beast is a survivor of the Age of Dinosaurs. If so, the beast would have witnessed the beginning of this separation of the continents, as it swam in the new Atlantic Ocean. But by the time Europe and North America were fully separated 70 million years ago, the beast would have been a lone survivor; the dinosaurs had long gone, and tiny furry mammals had begun their ascendancy.

The glen was still being molded by the violence of lava and sculpted by the gentle flows of water when modern man began his rise many hundreds of thousands of years ago. By this time, the Great Glen Fault had been subject to ages of strains from a heaving earth. Its sides had scraped past one another, back and forth like a giant grinding his teeth, until one side had moved 65 miles to the left of the other.

The fault was still a narrow gorge, and one more gigantic change was needed before the glen would be ready to receive the beast, then roaming the oceans, and the people, then huddled in caves in other lands. As the atmosphere cooled 25,000 years ago in the last ice age, thousands of feet of ice formed over the glen fault. The massive glaciers inched down the rift valley to the sea, gouging and carving the narrow gorge into the deep U-shaped bowl that would hold Loch Ness. As the glaciers began their slow, halting retreat, the flowing meltwaters and ice left a legacy of dramatically carved gorges, deep, rich soil and, most importantly, the Ness valley.

The sea seeped into the valley, and with it came the sea creatures, perhaps even the beast itself. The beast was attracted into the loch by the plentiful salmon that ventured in from the sea and swam up the many rivers to spawn and to escape their enemies. To the beast it was easier to hunt the salmon at the mouths of rivers than to chase them about in the open ocean.

The seas rose because of the added water from the melted glaciers. The land, relieved of its burden of ice, also rose. In the race between land and sea, the land won, and the loch became isolated from the sea, its inflowing rivers and streams gradually turning it to freshwater. The beast remained and adapted to the change; it was worth the effort to remain in the safe loch surrounded by plentiful food.

The people may have taken longer to discover the glen's advantages. Perhaps not until 6,000 years ago did they enter the Great Glen. The early settlers had almost certainly sailed their wood-framed cattle-hide boats across the Irish Sea into the sea of Loch Linnhe, and along the narrow string of lochs of the glen into Loch Ness. After the treacherous sea crossing and the treks between the lochs, Loch Ness must have looked inviting. The high walls of the loch gave little choice but to sail all the way up the loch to the flat lands around Inverness. The huge loch gave shelter from the cold, harsh climate of the Highlands, warming the winters and cooling the summers. It also afforded a transportation route and a rich source of fish. Deer, rabbits, and squirrels offered meat, and there were few other predators in the huge, dark forests to compete for the prey. Although the game was there to be hunted, the settlers were mainly farmers and herdsmen, attracted by the fields around the northeastern end of the loch and the rich deltas where meandering streams had eaten down the loch's high walls. The plentiful rains, rich soil, and long days of summer made for excellent farming in lush fields.

The settlers found a land that could afford them a living, but only by unremitting hard work. They were constantly reminded of the supremacy of nature. They were buffeted by the stark bone-chilling winds, and oppressed by the almost constant darkness of winter. Even in summer, the damp, almost-alive swirling mists often obscured the sun, making their world one of half-light. They witnessed the awesome displays of the northern lights in the winter sky and the deadly whims of the deep loch. There were sudden storms that could swamp boats, leaving the survivors to perish in the frigid waters. There were even tidal waves arising from earth tremors that shook the land.

The settlers were not beaten by the hardness around them, but it humbled them. They learned to live with nature, and to respect it, but to fight forever to keep it from at least a small, indomitable place in their spirits.

They saw that the rocks were as unyielding as they themselves would have to be, and they piled the round stones into circles to make places of worship. They built burial chambers of stone slabs in the midst of the circles and left their dead in the rooms, scattering small white pebbles as part of the magic. From the chambers of the dead would come human bones for dark rituals aimed at appeasing the powers around them. The overpowering land would soon erase most of the signs of the ancients, but their stone rings would remain as reminders of the early darkness.

The early inhabitants knew the loch well, and they must certainly have known the beast. The animal may even have entered into their religion, as did the many other natural forces surrounding them. A beast so sinister and so huge may have provoked a sinister and drastic magic to repel it. Perhaps even human lives were considered necessary sacrifices to appease the beast, and hints of such sacrifices occasionally surface in histories, as vague references to half-remembered events.

The early days of the Great Glen were marked by the violence of human against human, and the code of the warrior is still widely respected and preserved. Strategic hills were turned into primitive wood and earthen forts, and later into impregnable stone castles. Territory was jealously guarded, and rivalries between closely knit clans were frequent. Tales of atrocities by the enemy found a smooth highway from person to person and were readily recorded as gospel and as important history.

The wars were but brief, orgasmic episodes amidst centuries of featureless, harsh existence. On the surface, they were wars of revenge for some personal or political affront—clan against clan, or Scotsman against Englishman. But always underneath the battles seemed unconsciously to be as much a blind flailing against nature, in revenge for the cold, the deprivation, the darkness.

There was the interminable uncertainty of planting and harvest, of preventing the constant pressure of the seasons from suffocating the spirit. Cattle died, crops froze, people succumbed, but each year there was always something to celebrate; some good fortune, some happy event, some triumph. The people savored each delight, drawing close together and supporting one another, isolated and independent from the outside world.

Around their smoky peat fires, they told the tales of their long history, many running hours upon end. A moral was always carefully blended in to make the tale useful in everyday life. Generation after generation passed along the spoken history, with a precision produced only by constant repetition over seemingly interminable winters. The tales often told of heroes and their daring acts, and of villains and their treachery. But there were also tales of the fearsome, mysterious creatures that haunted the settlers' world, poised to endanger. There were the unpredictable fairies, who could sour milk, kidnap beautiful babies, or confuse men's minds. There were the *cailleachs*, or witches, who could be made to do good deeds, but had to be fought and subdued. And there was the kelpie, that evil spirit that haunted lonely lochs, waiting. . . .

The kelpie, or water-horse, was invariably evil, and the old stories tell of its wicked deeds, and of the humans who fought it. The kelpie, *Each Uisge* in Gaelic, lured its victims to their doom either by fascination or by mysterious powers, often assuming human form to work its evil. The horrible creature was an excellent vehicle for stamping a moral onto the mind of an impressionable youth:

Once, it is said, a kelpie in the form of a handsome young man made love to a farmer's daughter who lived near Loch Ness. His smooth talk overpowered the maiden, and she submitted to his advances. One day, however, she accidentally spilled boiling water on his foot, and the young man, rather than yelling in pain, whinnied like a horse. The maiden's brothers, upon hearing of the incident, attacked the young man, beating him viciously; whereupon, kicking and whinnying, he changed into a horse. Upon returning the next day to bury the horse, they discovered it gone, and a trail of slime leading into the loch.

Many Highland lochs have been believed to harbor the magical creatures, which were usually described as possessing long necks, humps, and a head resembling a horse or cow. In a popularity contest for water-monster havens, the isolated Loch Morar would undoubtedly run a close second to Loch Ness. Loch Ness is magnificent, but Loch Morar is eerily enchanting. The craggy mist-encircled mountains, crystal-clear water, and abrupt, huge island hummocks made Loch Morar an even more appropriate repository than Loch Ness for myth. It is here that a monster is said to dwell whose very sight portends death for a member of the clan MacDonnell. An old Scottish song captures the sense of dread:

> Morag, Harbinger of Death,
> Giant Swimmer in deep-green Morar
> The loch that has no bottom. . . .
> There it is that Morag the monster lives. . . .

There are stories to be told of water horses and their evil deeds, in countless lochs with names that roll richly off the tongue—Garloch, Lochaber, Lochfyne, Loch Awe, Loch na Mna, and of course Loch na Bieste—"Loch of the Beast."

(Scotland isn't the only home of long-necked, humped water monsters. The "loughs" of Ireland are also said to contain large unknown animals, as are cold, isolated lakes in Scandinavia, Russia, Canada, and the United States.)

In a 1527 history of Scotland by Hector Boece, it is told "that out of Garloch, a loch of Argyle came a terrible beast as big as a greyhound, puted like a gander and struck down great trees with the length of its tail; and slew three men quickly who were hunting, with three strokes of his tail."

And in Lochfyne in 1570, it is recorded in a Scottish history, the *Chronicles of Fortingale*: "There was ane monstrous fish . . . having a great een in the head thereof and at times would stand above the water as high as the mast of a ship; and the said had upon the head thereof twa croons [crowns]. . . ."

Whatever the water-horse, tales of it were told with conviction, so much so that, according to John Francis Campbell, a 19th-century collector of Scottish folk tales, "I have been told of English sportsmen who went in pursuit of them, so circumstantial were the accounts of those who believed they had seen them. The witnesses are so numerous, and their testimony agrees so well, that there must be some deeply-rooted Celtic belief which clothes with the dreaded form of the *Each Uisge* every dark object."

The confusion of dark stories of water horses may contain accounts of real unknown animals, but they are likely mixed with stories of seals, otters, and imaginary creatures. Nevertheless, the tales are gleefully harvested and picked over by modern monster-hunters in their researches. For instance, much is made of the entry on a 17th-century map which declares that Loch Lomond possesses "waves without wind, fish without fin, and a floating island."

Modern devotees of the beast take this to refer, respectively, to the huge wakes left by the creatures on calm lochs, the finless nature of the beast, and the fact that its hump may resemble an island. Perhaps so, but the 17th-century map also adds: "The fish that they speak of as having no fin are a kind of snake, and therefore no wonder." Could this mean an eel? And could the waves be nothing more than waves, and the islands, floating vegetation?

Perhaps more trustworthy is the common tale said to be the first record of the beast in Loch Ness. Saint Columba, the priest credited with bringing the Christian religion to northern Scotland, was said to have encountered a water beast in the loch during his travels. His biography, written in 565 A.D. by St. Adamnan, tells in Book 2, Chapter 27, "Of the Driving Away of a Certain Water Monster by Virtue of Prayer of the Holy Man." Says the account:

> At another time, again when the blessed man was staying for some days in the province of the Picts, he found it necessary to cross the River Ness; and when he came to the bank thereof, he sees some of the inhabitants burying a poor unfortunate man, whom, as those who were burying themselves reported, some water monster had, a little before, snatched at as he was swimming and bitten with a most savage bite, and whose hapless corpse some men who came in a boat to give assistance, though too late, caught hold of by putting out hooks. The blessed man, however, on hearing this, directs that some one of his companions shall swim out and bring to him the boat that is on the other side, sailing it across. On hearing this direction of the holy and famous man, Lugne Mocumin, obeying without delay, throws off all his clothes except his undergarment, and casts himself into the water. Now the Monster, which was not so much satiated as made eager for prey, was lying hid in the bottom of the river; but perceiving

that the water above was disturbed by him who was crossing, suddenly emerged, and swimming to the man as he was crossing in the middle of the stream, rushed up with a great roar and open mouth.

Then the blessed man looked on, while all who were there, the heathen as well as the brethren, were stricken with very great terror; and with his holy hand raised on high he formed the sign of the cross in the empty air, invoked the name of God, and commanded the fierce monster, saying,—Think not to go further nor touch thou that man. Quick go back! Then the beast on hearing this voice of the saint, was terrified and fled backwards more rapidly than he came, as if dragged by cords, although it had come so near to Lugne as he swam, that there was not more than the length of a punt pole between the man and the beast. Then the brethren, seeing that the beast had gone away and that their comrade Lugne was returned to them safe and sound in the boat, glorified God in the blessed man, greatly marvelling. Moreover also the barbarous heathen who were there present, constrained by the greatness of the miracle, which they themselves had seen, glorified the God of the Christians.

Of course the biography was not written until a century after Columba's death, and is a frankly adoring account replete with many miracles and fabulous stories. In his time, according to Adamnan, Columba busied himself by raising folk from the dead, curing all manner of ills, sailing against the wind, and magically opening locked gates. No wonder that he should also battle a water monster.

But there are problems for those who would disbelieve that this story is about a real beast. Adamnan pointedly asserts the veracity of his work: "Let no one imagine that I either state a falsehood regarding so great a man, or record anything doubtful or uncertain," he wrote. "Be it known that I will tell with all candor what I have learned from the consistent narrative of my predecessors, trustworthy and discerning men, and that my narrative is founded either on what I have been able to find recorded in the pages of those who have gone before me, or what I have learned on diligent inquiry, by hearing it from certain faithful old men, who have told me without hesitation."

The faithful biographer also stuck closely to real animals and real objects throughout his narrative, so whether Columba actually encountered the beast or not, Adamnan may still be referring to a flesh-and-blood creature in the story. Maybe Adamnan, or his sources, did stray a little from the truth . . . just this once. And maybe he didn't.

In the ancient tales, the kelpie as an evil spirit and the kelpie as a real animal were inextricably intertwined, woven together by generations of storytelling. The weaving was understandable; the real beast would have been a rare creature, infrequently sighted. Perfectly natural, then, that it would remain on the border between reality and legend.

The isolation of the Highlands and the reticence of its people tightened the protective cover of myth thrown over the beast. But the cover was imperfect, for through the years, the stories of water horses began to acquire an uncomfortable tinge of reality.

On March 6, 1856, *The Times of London* reported soberly: "The village of Leurbost, Parish of Lochs, Lewis, is at present the scene of an unusual occurrence. This is no less than the appearance in one of the inland freshwater lakes of an animal which from its great size and dimensions has not a little puzzled our island naturalists. Some suppose him to be a description of the hitherto mythological water-kelpie. . . . It has been repeatedly seen within the last fortnight by crowds of people, many of whom have come from the remotest parts of Scotland to witness the uncommon spectacle. The animal is described by some as being in appearance and size like 'a large peat stack,' while others affirm that a 'six-oared boat' could pass between the huge fins which are occasionally visible. All, however, agree as describing its form as that of an eel; and we have heard one whose evidence we can rely on, state that in length it supposed it to be 40 feet. It is probable that this is no more than a conger eel after all, animals of this description having been caught in Highland lakes which have attained huge size."

At Loch Ness, stories of the beast were rare—the loch had no roads near it and was the realm only of fishermen and local farmers. But there were reports. A farmer, Alexander MacDonald said that one day in 1802 as he was rescuing a lamb on the shore, he had seen a large animal surface and propel itself to within 50 yards of him with short, stubby appendages.

Then there was the story of Duncan MacDonald, who in 1880 dove to inspect a shipwreck near the Fort Augustus entrance to the Caledonian Canal. After frantically signaling to be pulled up, he emerged from the water pale and trembling, and only after a few days had passed would tell his story. He had been examining the keel of the ship when he had seen a huge animal lying on a rock shelf that held the wreck. He had described the beast as looking like a huge frog, and he vowed never to dive in the loch again.

The Inverness Courier reported a 1926 sighting of Mr. Simon McGarry of Invergarry. He had been watching gulls skimming the surface of the loch near Cherry Island at the Fort Augustus end of the loch, when suddenly the gulls rose screaming into the air. "Then, before my eyes, something like a large upturned boat rose from the depths, and I can still see the water cascading down its sides," he was quoted as saying. "Just as suddenly, though, it sank out of sight, but it was an extraordinary experience."

The reports continued to surface occasionally here and there, as did the beast, until two events transformed the animal into an international celebrity. The first was the construction of Highway A82, blasted out of rock along the northern shore of the loch. The highway construction involved clearance of a considerable amount of undergrowth, so it gave travelers an excellent view of the loch. The other event was the first sensational press account of the "Loch Ness Monster" published in 1933 in the *Inverness Courier*. The sighting of Mr. and Mrs. John McKay of "an enormous animal rolling and plunging" in the loch set off the great media marathon that continues today.

🌣 Chapter Six

THE BEAST

The discovery of the beast by the media began a steady flow of sighting reports, hoaxes, and grandly conceived expeditions to solve the mystery "once and for all." For the next half century, the beast sailed mysteriously, tantalizingly through the lives of thousands of people who saw it, photographed it, or pursued it—farmers, game-keepers, policemen, scientists, fishermen, physicians, priests, beggars, drunks, men, women, children, and even dogs. None were the same after the experience.

With the beast's introduction to the outside world came the appellation "monster," pinned on it by the newspapers. The Scots had never called the animal in the loch a monster, not even in its dark history as an evil myth. It was simply a part of nature—a "beast." Never was it abnormal or deviant—a "monster." Even today, the Scots dislike the term "monster" for the animal that has touched their lives for so many centuries. The media have even given the beast a personality, nicknaming it Nessie, and cartooning it as a peaceful, friendly creature. If it has any personality trait, the beast certainly has a perverse sense of humor—those who have sought it have been, with some exceptions, abysmally unsuccessful, while many an unsuspecting soul going about his daily business has been treated to a frightening close-up of the beast.

The total store of data gathered by organized expeditions to the loch could be comfortably borne by a medium-sized house cat. But the accounts of those expeditions make a delicious collection of the vagaries of human nature. Excitement, fear, boredom, frustration, and greed are excellent stimulants; they bring out a zoo of little hidden human quirks.

The tone for "scientific studies" of the beast was set by the first highly publicized loch adventure in 1933. Sponsored by the *Daily Mail*, big-game hunter M. A. Wetherall arrived at the Loch in December of that year, vowing to track down "Nessie." Only a few days after Wetherall's arrival, the *Mail* trumpeted the hunter's discovery of large footprints of the beast on the shore of the loch. They quoted Wetherall: "It is a four-fingered beast and it has feet or pads about eight inches across. I should judge it to be a very powerful soft-footed animal about 20 feet long. The spoor I have found clearly shows the undulations of the pads and outlines of the claws and nails. . . . I am convinced it can breathe like a hippopotamus or crocodile with just one nostril out of the water.

"The spoor I found is only a few hours old, clearly demonstrating that the animal is in the neighborhood where I expected to find it."

Plaster casts of the tracks were dispatched to the British Museum of Natural History; and the world, the press, and Wetherall waited breathlessly for the results. They were worth waiting for, if only because of the grand joke.

"We are unable to find any significant difference between these impressions and those made by the foot of a hippopotamus," concluded the museum report. "The closest agreement is with the right hind foot of a mounted specimen. . . ." The "creature" had been a hippopotamus umbrella stand owned by a resident of the area.

More serious was a 1934 expedition sponsored by a well-to-do insurance executive, Sir Edward Mountain, who stationed 20 unemployed men with cameras and binoculars around the loch for five weeks. The results were 11 reasonably good sightings; one close enough for the observer to report a head resembling a goat's, with two stumps on top resembling broken-off sheep's horns. The detailed description included a dark brown color, front flippers, and eyes shaped like slits.

Throughout the 1940s and 1950s and into the 1960s the beast—or rather those who saw it—was pursued only by the media. The newspapers usually punctuated their reports of sightings with giggles and flourishes of journalistic wit, dubbing the beast a silly-season phenomenon. Book authors were more circumspect—if not defensive—

about the animal. In 1957 Constance Whyte, a retired physician who was the wife of the Caledonian Ship Canal manager, made a powerful case for the animal in her influential book *More Than a Legend*; and in the 1960s Tim Dinsdale carefully chronicled his exploits in *Loch Ness Monster* and other books. It was Constance Whyte's book, bought on a vacation trip to Scotland, that first introduced Rines to the incredible idea that there might really be a giant beast in the loch.

The 1970s saw the continuation of the ironic trend of serious books written about a beast the rest of the world considered a joke. In 1974 Nicholas Witchell published an account of the beast's history in *The Loch Ness Story*, and in 1975 biochemist Roy P. Mackal presented the scientific evidence in *The Monsters of Loch Ness*.

Mackal had been involved in the 1960s expeditions of the Loch Ness Investigation Bureau—the most serious and long-term effort to solve the mystery since the beast's discovery by the outside world. The bureau was founded by a group including Constance Whyte, Sir Peter Scott, and David James. Beginning in 1962, the bureau sponsored expeditions including every trick and technological gadget the dedicated amateurs could dream up. Immense searchlights were placed over the dark loch to attract the beast; a homemade submarine dove in search of it; an autogyro patrolled the air above the loch hoping for a glimpse; underwater microphones listened for its voice. But the major effort of the hundreds of volunteers over the decade of expeditions was to man large camera rigs fitted with powerful long-range lenses. Bureau volunteers camped in trailers and tents in a field at Achnahannet, dispersing during the day to numerous camera sites around the loch.

It was a frustrating vigil, and the beast's orneriness won in the end. The few sightings they did have of the animal occurred when fog or poor light prevented filming. Or else the sightings were too near shore for the camera to record—some of the camera stations were set back on mountains overlooking the loch, and near-shore vision was obstructed by the mountain. The amateurs were mainly college students and, at least once, amatory exploration prevented zoological exploration. One long-time resident, Mrs. Winifred Cary recalls that one time she spied the beast above water, rushed over to the nearest bureau camera site, and found the students on duty locked in a passionate embrace. Perhaps they weren't body and soul for science, but only soul.

The results of a decade's effort by the bureau and others were inconclusive. There were sonar contacts with large underwater moving objects, film footage of several mysterious wakes and disturbances, and recordings from underwater microphones of unidentified, but perhaps animate sounds. Nevertheless, the results and the bureau's collection of sighting reports did attract other technologists to the cause.

Always there was Tim Dinsdale. Since 1960 he had haunted the loch, watching from the shore, or drifting silently in his boat. He was an indefatigable, thorough, good-humored pursuer of the beast. He was always available to aid expeditions even going along with the more bizarre experiments—*anything* to find the beast. In one experiment to lure the animal with sound transmitted underwater, Dinsdale chose Beethoven's Sixth Symphony (The "Pastoral") and lounged in his boat happily bombarding the inconsiderate, intransigent creature with the magnificent strains.

Since his persuasive 1960 film of the beast, Dinsdale had seen it only twice more in all his years on the loch—in 1970 and 1971. Both sightings were of the neck poking out of the water, but at neither time did he have a chance to take pictures. The 1971 sighting was perhaps the most frustrating. It was September 6 and Dinsdale was plowing his boat through the rough waters of the loch, when, "Out of the corner of my eye I spotted a black snakelike object rear above the water; it stayed erect for a moment, then it was quickly withdrawn. By now I was staring full-face spellbound toward the object——unbelieving. Surely it *couldn't* be the monster. After so many fruitless years of searching, my mind simply rejected the possibility.

"I continued to stare, only to see it again break surface, then go down in a boil of foam." The frustrated Dinsdale had been so mesmerized by the sight that he had been unable to use his camera.

The bureau closed its operations in 1972. Ironically, it was the same year that Rines' underwater flipper photograph gave the first close-up of the beast and opened a whole new technological toolbox for monster-hunters.

The monster-hunters badly needed to find better methods. So far, the only requirement proven necessary to encounter the beast had been a good supply of dumb luck. The main body of evidence for the creature was the thousands of inadvertent sightings and few accidental photographs obtained when average people blundered into the beast.

Sometimes the blundering was inopportune for the people as well as the animal. One photograph of the beast which attracted widespread attention is said to have been taken while the photographer was on a jaunt with a lady not his wife.

For Alex Campbell, the water bailiff who had seen the beast many times, one particular encounter, in the mid–1950s was especially inconvenient. He was rowing out into the middle of the loch one calm summer day, when suddenly the boat began to heave underneath him. Campbell's dog leaped under the seat quivering, as a terrified Campbell tried to control the boat. "It is the only time I have ever felt frightened on the loch in my whole life," he said. "Believe me, I put my back into the oars to get away from the spot—I didn't even dare to move to the stern to start the motor." Campbell's was not the only encounter on the water. There have been other reports over the years of fishermen appearing at a local bar, shaking, very quiet, and downing several more drinks than their usual. After such fortification, they would invariably tell a tale of a calm evening, a quiet casting for fish, and sudden panic at an abrupt splashing up from the depths of a huge hump, or a neck and head.

By far most of the sightings over the decades have been of the beast's huge hump, sometimes two, sometimes three. The hump has been seen at some times speeding down the loch, throwing up a powerful wake, at others abruptly surfacing, with water cascading from its flanks. Many other sightings have been of the snakelike head and neck, usually protruding several feet out of the water. Sometimes the hump followed behind it on the surface, sometimes not. Sometimes the head and neck moved down the loch; sometimes it remained stationary, swaying nervously from side to side.

But these generalities do not really capture the feeling of the sightings, the sheer horror of those who have seen the beast close up, or the utter fascination of those who have seen it from a distance. The only way to understand the human reaction is to tell some of the stories, to take a trip in time and space around the loch. If we were to squeeze into a single instant the thousands of encounters between man and the beast, the shores and waters of the loch and even the surrounding roads, would become a writhing mass of heads, necks, humps, people, boats, cameras, cars, even motorcycles. Sightings have occurred everywhere, under all circumstances. We'll choose only a few, admittedly the more exciting. The accounts seem reliable, but there could be a few tall stories mixed in. But even if only some of these tales are true, then the animal must exist.

Begin the trip at Temple Pier, Urquhart Bay, the base for so many monster-hunting expeditions. The traveler on the road beside the loch has but a brief glimpse of Urquhart Bay, and the castle on the opposite shore, before the road north curves immediately away from the loch. It winds past rich farms stretching away on the hills above and below the road, and it curves down among the neat, modest cottages of Drumnadrochit. The road crosses the rivers Enrick and Coiltie and shoots across the low green river valley to approach the loch again on the other side of the bay. The road curves around the mountainside jutting out into the loch, overlooking the jumbled ruin of Urquhart Castle on the promontory below. Here the stories of sightings shall begin in a rather grand manner, as

THE BEAST IS WITNESSED BY A MULTITUDE. On October 8, 1936, two busloads and several carloads of people watched the beast disport itself in the loch for a full 15 minutes. One Duncan MacMillan, whose cottage was perched above the road, first saw a head and neck rise magnificently out of the calm loch about 500 yards from shore. As the beast moved along slowly, people began to gather at the roadside, buses pulled up, and the crowd swelled to about 50. Telescopes and binoculars were trained on the amazing sight, and witnesses described how two humps surfaced behind the head and neck. And then quickly the beast was gone.

Over the years since then other tour bus passengers and sometimes entire busloads have glimpsed humps or heads and necks splashing along in the loch. There is one amusing story—probably apocryphal—of a tour-bus director who saw the head and neck of the beast moving majestically down the loch, and announced calmly to the passengers of his bus: "I know it's not a part of the itinerary, but if you look to the left you'll see the Loch Ness monster." Thirty passengers, presumably with 30 cameras, looked to the left and got an excellent view of the monster. But nobody took a picture! After all, it wasn't on the itinerary.

The traveler journeys only a little further along the highway toward Alltsigh before the next sighting area. The right side of the road is hemmed in by a sheer rock cliff, while the loch, and the narrow beach below are only occasionally visible behind a thick screen of trees and underbrush. It was here that occurred

THE ADVENTURE OF THE ENGINEER. A. H. Palmer, an electrical engineer in the area on business, had spent the night of August 11, 1933, in his car near the shore, when at 7:00 A.M. he heard a huge rush of water on the still loch. He investigated, but saw only waves

mouth open
12-18 ins. wide.
red inside

Very flat head with hornlike
projections

The head seen on the surface of the loch by A. H. Palmer in 1933. (*Dinsdale: Loch Ness Monster*)

breaking on the shore; apparently from something that moved past his vantage point down the loch. But it hadn't been a boat; he would have seen it, for it had taken only a moment to reach the water's edge.

An hour later he returned to the shore, and saw, about 100 yards out "a flat head on the surface which appeared like a very shallow inverted bowl and almost black in color."

In a letter to author Rupert Gould, Palmer described the head: "At each side I saw a short antenna which I can best describe as being like the horns on the head of a snail. Between them was a wide mouth opening and closing at about two-second intervals. The width of the mouth I should estimate at about 12–18 inches, and it opened to the extent of about six inches.

"It appeared to be steadily breathing or basking on the surface, and remained so for at least half an hour, gradually drifting in a south-easterly direction toward the far bank." Business called, and Palmer left the beast lying peacefully on the surface.

The road down the loch continues, passing small cottages and a campground below on the loch. It is but a few miles to the field at Achnahannet where the Loch Ness Investigation Bureau had its base. The loch is a featureless expanse of water with shores almost unbroken by bays and inlets. Once Urquhart Bay is left behind, the loch seems to have little that would draw the beast to the surface. But humps have been seen from this stretch of road, and in 1967 Dorothy Fraser, who lives in a cottage above the road, saw "a big gray-black oval mass" rise from the depths, gather speed out into the loch, and suddenly sink, leaving its ob-server quite weak in the knees.

Most of the sightings, however, have been near the mouths of streams. No one knows whether this concentration is due to the animal's habits or because there are simply more humans near river mouths to see the animals. Farther down the road at Alltsigh a small stream runs under the road and into the loch. It was near "Alltsigh Burn" that occurred the sighting of

THE FEEDING BEAST. One day in June 1938, John MacLean was standing near the mouth of the burn, considering the possibility of a little fishing, when the head and neck of the beast suddenly reared up less than 20 yards away. "It was without any doubt in the act of swallowing food," he told a local newspaper. "It opened and closed its mouth several times quite quickly and then kept tossing its head backward in exactly the same manner as a cormorant does after it has devoured a fish." The beast then dived, two distinct humps and a length of tail breaking the surface behind it. It surfaced again further away and then slowly sank. MacLean described in detail the animal that had left him "petrified with astonishment."

"The monster, I am sure is 18 to 20 feet long, the tail fully six feet, and the largest hump was about three feet high. The head is small and pointed, the skin very dark brown on the back and like that of a horse when wet and glistening. The neck is thin and several feet long, but I saw no flippers or fins."

Beyond Alltsigh Burn, the road leaves the loch briefly, to pass through the tiny village of Invermoriston. The traveler comes to a crossroad and turns left to head out of the thick woods and back onto the shore of the loch. It was on this stretch of road that one monster-hunter experienced

A BUSY, BUSY DAY. Early on the morning of July 8, 1975, teacher Allen Wilkins and his son Ian were scanning the surface of the loch from a point about 1½ miles south of Invermoriston. The loch was a flat gray calm surface. At 7:20 Wilkins saw a dark line materialize off a promontory far down the loch. It sank and reappeared several times as he watched. Then an abrupt black shape rose out of the water, only to disappear and then reappear as a dark line once more before it finally submerged. Wilkins estimated the line to be about 20 feet long and about two feet out of the water.

But Allen Wilkins' day was not over. At 10:12 he photographed in the same area what he believed to be an inflatable black boat tearing about the loch under motorpower. But his wife, upon examining the object, declared it was no boat but a large hump, which sank and reappeared as three humps. Others nearby had also begun watching the strange phenomenon, and agreed that there were three triangular humps playing about in the loch. A jet fighter thundered dramatically overhead, but the humps remained. Only when a motor yacht approached did they finally disappear.

Allen Wilkins' day was still not over. That evening, at 9:25, at the same position, he spied a black patch on the surface in the same area as his earlier sighting. The water seemed to be boiling around the patch. Wilkins had just called the attention of fellow watchers to the disturbance, when they all saw two angular humps emerging majestically from the loch, like a whale surfacing. Seconds later the humps sank, with the suggestion of a slow forward roll.

Allen Wilkins' day was *still* not over. At 10:25 P.M. one of the watchers called the group's attention to three closely spaced humps, about four feet high, moving out of nearby Invermoriston Bay, about one mile away. As they moved, the humps turned, each in imitation of the hump ahead, altering from three to two humps and back several times. The watchers called out in unison as the number of humps changed. Then they were gone. *Now* Allen Wilkins' day was over. He had witnessed perhaps a record number of separate sightings in one day, and they were classic, unequivocal sightings. The humps had submerged and resurfaced many times, proving they were not birds. They had not gone near land, and had finally submerged permanently, proving they were not otters or other land animals. They had moved rapidly through the water, proving they weren't merely floating masses of vegetation, rarely seen in the loch anyway. Finally, the sightings had been witnessed by others and recorded on film. A busy, busy day.

About a mile farther on, the traveler reaches the area of another important sighting, in which

THE ARTIST MEETS THE BEAST. Torquil MacLeod was a full-time monster-hunter and trained artist, sponsored by a wealthy patron. On February 28, 1960, a dull, drizzly day, he had pulled up beside the road briefly on a trip south from Invermoriston, when an object caught his eye on the opposite shore of the loch. He focused his binoculars on the area, and saw a large dark mass moving about on the steep shore, at the water's edge. At the front he saw what looked like a weaving, outsized elephant's trunk, and paddles were visible on both sides of the bulky body. He wrote later to Tim Dinsdale that "For about 8 or 9 minutes the animal remained quite still, but for its 'trunk' (I assume neck, although I could not recognize a head as such) which occasionally moved from side to side with a slight up and down motion—just like a snake about to strike. . . .

"In the end it made a sort of half jump-half lurch to the left, its 'trunk' coming right around until it was facing me, then it flopped into the water and apparently went straight down; so it must be very deep close inshore at that point."

It was a frustrating sighting because nobody else could have seen the beast from the opposite shore—the road was far back from the loch. Also, MacLeod had no telephoto lens, and his binoculars were not strong enough to pick out details of the head. But the careful monster-hunter pinpointed his location and that of the beast, and calculated the beast's length from this information, map measurements, and the scale markings on the lens of his binoculars. He arrived at the remarkable figure of 45 feet, and allowing for the angle of the body away from him, the beast could have been more than 50 feet long. And this was just the portion out of water! The beast, if that long, would have qualified fully for the title "water-bull," which legend bestowed upon especially large beasts in Scottish lochs. MacLeod made careful drawings of what he saw, depicting a huge, swaying body moving ponderously about on the shore.

MacLeod's sighting is significant because it is the only major land sighting since the earliest days of the beast's popularity, in the 1930s. Monster-hunters attribute the plentitude of early land sightings to the lack of noise and traffic around the loch, a situation drastically changed with the completion of the highway on the northern shore.

> As the traveler ventures farther down the road, he approaches the southern tip of the narrow loch, one of the richest areas of sightings. At Fort Augustus, where the rivers Tarff and Oich and the Caledonian Canal feed into the loch, many have seen the beast splashing about fishing, and even basking on land. Also in the small town is the Benedictine Abbey at Fort Augustus, an 18th-century fortress converted into a magnificent, peaceful place of God. Many monks have witnessed surfacings from the vantage point of the tree-covered grounds of the abbey, which overlook the length of the loch stretching away into the distance. We shall call one of the most recent sightings

THE PRIEST'S ENCOUNTER. Father Gregory Brusey is a warm, humorous, gentle man, and delights in showing visitors through the abbey. After a few charming stories about the antics of the boys at the abbey school, he also likes to tell of his encounter with the beast on October 14, 1971. It was a fine, sunny morning and he was showing a visitor the lovely view of the placid loch, when they were both startled by a terrific commotion in the waters below the abbey. About 300 yards away, amidst the disturbance, they saw the head and neck of the creature, rising to a height of about seven feet. It swam slowly away from the two men, its neck at a slight angle and submerged after about 20 seconds. "We felt a sort of awe and amazement. In fact, my friend said if I hadn't been with him he'd probably have run," said Father Gregory. "It gave us a feeling of something from another world."

It is a magic moment when Father Gregory tells of his experience. The quiet certainty of this gentle cleric in his simple brown robes seems more powerful evidence for the existence of the beast than any photographic image. The complex intellectual wrangling over the beast seems pallid in comparison with this one calmly told story of a 20-second episode.

Of the many fascinating accounts of sightings near Fort Augustus, there is another we should tell—the story of

THE MAID AND THE BEAST. Margaret Munro was a young maid in the service of Kilchumein Lodge just west of Fort Augustus. Early on the morning of June 3, 1934, she was busy about her duties when she happened to glance out of the dining room window toward the loch. About 300 yards away, on the rocky shore, she was astounded to see a large creature lolling about. She took up a pair of binoculars, and for about 25 minutes watched the creature enjoy the sun. It was, she said, the largest creature she had ever seen, with a "giraffe-like neck and absurdly small head out of all proportions to the great dark body, skin like an elephant and two very short forelegs or flippers." The animal turned one way and then another, enjoying the sun, and finally slipped quietly back into the loch. Being a good servant, Miss Munro did not wake her masters with such a triviality.

From the abbey, the narrow road loops around the tip of the loch and begins to climb into the Highlands. The traveler leaves the loch for a while, for the single-lane road arches up over the rim of the valley and across the barren heath. In this long loop away from the loch, the traveler comes to understand how much of a sanctuary the Great Glen really is, for the Highlands are far less inviting away from the loch. The rock outcrops and scrub decorate the land bleakly. There is water, to be sure—the modest Loch Tarff and meandering streams—but they seem to flow through the country without stopping to give moisture to the land.

Traveling through the barren Highlands, one realizes how much the loch is a gigantic natural aquarium—a safe, sheltered environment. Its waters are purified and aerated in their passage through the mountains. The salmon and other migrating fish are contributed by the sea, to be a principal food source for the loch's denizens. Even the lush farms on its hillside seem to have been laid out by a tasteful landscape architect concerned with creating a place of sanctuary.

After several miles of rough Highland landscape, the road curves back to the loch, running alongside the deep gorge of the Foyers

River. The road zigzags back and forth up a hill, until once more at Foyers the loch comes into view. Down this hill a bit is the spot where Tim Dinsdale obtained his remarkable film of the beast splashing through the waters on the far side of the loch. It was

THE BIRTH OF A MONSTER-HUNTER. After carefully studying the evidence gathered about the beast, Dinsdale set forth in the spring of 1960 from his home in Reading, England, with camera equipment and camping gear to investigate the story firsthand. On the morning of April 20, 1960, he had been watching the loch since dawn and was heading for breakfast at Foyers. Fortunately, on his trip to the nearby hotel, he stuck firmly to his discipline of always being at the ready when in sight of the loch, stopping to set up his camera in his car before proceeding down the hill overlooking the water. No sooner had he come in sight of the loch than he saw an object moving about across the loch at a distance of about 1,800 yards. He trained his binoculars on the object and saw a long, oval reddish-brown hump, with a dark blotch on the side, like the dappling on a cow. As it began to move, he began to film. It zigzagged across the loch, leaving a definite wake, and slowly submerged. Even traveling submerged, the beast still left a wake, as well as rhythmic paddle strokes, "pure white blobs of froth contrasting starkly against the black water," said Dinsdale. Gambling on getting into a better position he raced his car down the hill to the lochside, only to find that the hump had gone without a trace.

"Through the magic lens of my camera I had reached out across the thousand yards and more, *to grasp the monster by the tail*," he later wrote. The beast had mesmerized another human.

There is another monster-hunter to be found here in Foyers, but by no means a friend of Dinsdale. Frank Searle camps down a winding side road on a flat beach beside the loch, and constantly scans the waters for a surfacing. He is a tourist attraction, the darling of the local press and hotel owners, drawing thousands of visitors a year, they say. A little blue shack holds the many mementos of his seven-year vigil on the loch—newspaper clippings, mimeographed newsletters, a box for accepting donations, and a collection of pictures of ungainly monsterlike objects on the water's surface. Searle stands with his cameras on the shore of the loch, posing with a dedicated set to his face, like a latter-day Captain Ahab. His round face, pencil-thin moustache, and deep sunburn, remind one of a Bronx barber just back from a week in Miami.

But he is a monster-hunter extraordinaire who deserted his job as a grocery-store manager to live a hermit's existence on the shore of the loch. The monster has become his quarry, his fascination, and a marvelous stepladder to a self-constructed ego pedestal.

It must have been a frustrating, lonely existence for Searle, living on the shore of the loch for so many years. And what luck to obtain a whole set of shots of the beast on October 21, 1972! Out in his little boat, he says, he saw the beast emerge from the loch only yards away (holding its mouth open, and posing sideways so he could photograph it). Then it submerged, came up on the other side, and posed again. In later versions of the pictures, it is said, the beast even added a hump. How nice. What luck, what fame, what fortune awaited because of those photographs of the angular object sitting leadenly in the water. Interviews by the press, radio, and television; documentaries; and even a post as official Loch Ness correspondent for the monster-crazy Japanese.

Even greater luck was to await the lone stalker of great beasts! One day in 1974, alone in his boat, he photographed a flying saucer speeding across the loch at about 2,000 feet! More publicity, more fame,

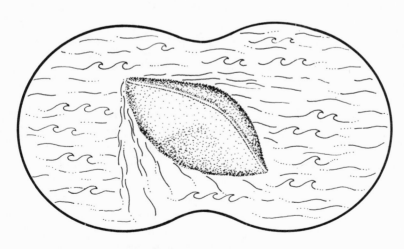

The hump filmed by Tim Dinsdale in 1960. (*Dinsdale: Loch Ness Monster*)

more money. Those others are fakers, hoaxsters, fools, he tells visitors—those Dinsdales and their unlikely films ("someday we'll know what he *really* filmed") and those Rineses and their questionable underwater photographs. And how ridiculous the conclusions by experts that his photographs are not only fakes, but poor fakes. The atmosphere around the strange, lonely man seems charged with vehemence, and the traveler retreats thankfully up the hill and back onto the main road.

Back to the sunlit road, which passes the village of Inverfarigaig, the traveler rounds a rock outcropping and descends almost to the level of the loch. Along this stretch of road occurred one of the most extraordinary reports of the beast on land:

WHY DOES A MONSTER CROSS THE ROAD? Driving south on this road, about 4:00 in the afternoon of July 22, 1933, were Mr. and Mrs. George Spicer, a vacationing company director and his wife. "What on earth is that?" Mrs. Spicer suddenly exclaimed, as they saw a huge form emerging from the bracken on the hillside 200 yards ahead and lurching clumsily across the road. "It was horrible—an abomination," Mr. Spicer recalled to a reporter. "First we saw an undulating sort of neck, a little thicker than an elephant's trunk. It did not move in the usual reptilian fashion but, with three arches in its neck, it shot across the road until a ponderous body about four feet high came into view."

The Spicers accelerated toward it, but it had vanished by the time they reached the spot, leaving only a gap in the undergrowth where it had passed. They hadn't noticed a head because the creature had crossed the road before they had realized what was happening.

"It had been a loathsome sight," said Spicer. "It seems futile to describe it because it was like nothing I have read about or seen. It was terrible. Its color, so far as the body was concerned, could be called a dark elephant gray. It looked like a huge snail with a long neck." Spicer estimated the length to be about 25 to 30 feet, and he worried that it could have upset the car, had he hit it. Upon discussing the incident later with author Rupert Gould, the new movie *King Kong* was mentioned. Spicer declared that the animal he had seen much resembled the diplodocus-like dinosaur in that movie, except that the neck was more flexible and no appendages were visible because the base of the

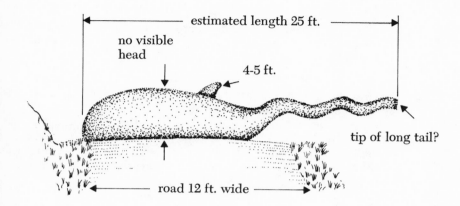

Sketch made under the direction of Mr. Spicer of the animal he and his wife saw crossing the road in front of their car in 1933. (*Dinsdale: Loch Ness Monster*)

animal was obscured by a dip in the road. Until that sighting, the Spicers said they had not known that the loch was supposed to harbor a mysterious creature.

The traveler continues the journey down the straight, narrow road, and into the village of Dores at the end of the loch. In the loch, just off Tor Point in Dores Bay, R. H. Lowrie had skewed about in his yacht attempting to avoid the frightening hump in his 1960 encounter. His adventure had been observed from the opposite shore by Torquil MacLeod and several companions.

The road winds into Inverness, where stone buildings and castle turrets line the River Ness, a straight, swift river running to the sea. It was in the center of town that occurred the encounter of

THE TWO BUSINESSMEN. On the stormy afternoon of July 30, 1965, Hamish Ferguson and George McGill were standing on the steps of the Inverness YMCA, when they saw coursing down the center of the river, three triangular humps, totaling about 15 feet in length. For about six minutes the men watched the black humps leave a trail of ripples as they moved down the river. Mr. Ferguson told the local newspaper: "This has absolutely amazed me. It was very much alive and for all the world like one of those prehistoric animals you see in picture books." One might normally suspect they had been tippling, but the two businessmen were not the first to see humps in the river. In June 1936, Mr. and Mrs. Hallam, on board a pleasure boat reported two humps, totaling about 20 feet, and a head, moving quickly down the river toward the sea.

> The traveler crosses the bridge in town and heads back south for several miles before starting down the north shore of the loch, heading back toward Temple Pier. Just past the beach and the cluster of white cottages at Lochend, the traveler passes Abriachan Pier, another rich area for sightings. Two of the most interesting sightings were decades apart; one in 1976 and one in 1934. The 1976 episode should rightly be called

THE WORLD CHAMPIONSHIP HUMP SIGHTING. It was a cool, rainy evening and the loch was calm on July 12, 1976. Two Inverness mechanics, Ian Dunn and Billy Kennedy, were puttering about one-quarter mile off Abriachan Pier, testing a newly repaired boat, when, turning to look at the wake the boat was leaving, they saw a hump about 200 yards behind them. The fascinated pair turned the boat about and went back for a better look, and found themselves amidst a confusion of five weaving, plunging humps, matte black in color, 10 to 12 feet long and two to three feet high. Dunn and Kennedy were frightened but exhilarated as the humps disappeared and surfaced around them. The possibility that one of the animals could overturn the boat prompted them to put on life jackets. The display lasted about 15 minutes, whereupon the men headed for shore. They had seen enough, and a rainstorm was moving down the loch toward them.

"It was like getting caught in the center of a school of whales," said Dunn. "They weren't scared of the sound of our engine. When we pulled away, one of them even followed us."

"I don't know what we saw," said Kennedy. "We could only make out the humps—but they definitely were not seals. They were too big, and if they had been seals, we would have seen their heads."

Dunn's and Kennedy's sighting offers the lesson—as have other multiple sightings—that there is more than one beast in the loch. In fact there must be a fairly large breeding herd for the beast to have survived thousands of years. Calculations of the number of beasts supportable by the loch's food supply show that up to 100 of the animals could survive on the fish and eels in the loch. However the magic number to most monster-hunters is 30, the minimum size for a viable population.

The other fascinating encounter near Abriachan Pier occurred on the road itself. This sighting should be known as the affair of

THE MIDNIGHT CYCLIST. On January 5, 1934, at 1:30 A.M., Arthur Grant, a young veterinary student was speeding along the loch road near Abriachan on his motorcycle, when he spotted a dark object beside the road about 40 yards ahead of him. It was a bright, moonlit night, so he could see the object well as his motorcycle sped toward it, and the beast bounded across the road and plunged into the loch with a loud splash. Grant leaped off his cycle and followed the creature, but by the time he reached the loch, he could see nothing but a disturbance in the water.

Grant had been so close to the beast that he had nearly struck it with his motorcycle. He had seen what he took to be a head turn toward him, which he said resembled that of a large eel, with oval eyes. And then, as the animal took flight, a bulky body with two slight humps, and a long tail, rounded at the end, and four flippers.

The creature was 15 to 20 feet long, and moved across the road using its flippers with a lope reminiscent of a sea lion.

Grant, a veterinary student with considerable knowledge of animals, declared, "I can say that I have never seen anything in my life like the animal I saw. It looked like a hybrid."

As with many witnesses, Grant was subjected to much ridicule because of his story; but also, as with many sightings, his story has outlived the ridicule.

> The road from Abriachan back to Temple Pier is high above the water, and the loch is often obscured by thick bushes. But there have been sightings here, too, of heads and necks emerging from the loch, water streaming down them, and of humps playing about on the surface. But we shall skip them, as we have skipped hundreds of other reputable recorded sightings. The trip is over. What have we learned?

With the photographs, sonar records, and the sightings lending support to the beast's reality, the question has become not whether the beast exists, but what is it?

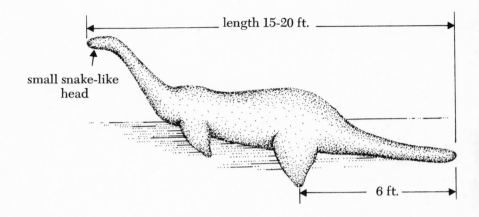

length 15-20 ft.

small snake-like
head

6 ft.

Veterinary student Arthur Grant sketched this drawing of the
creature he encountered the night of January 5, 1934. (Shape of
limbs indefinite.) (*Dinsdale: Loch Ness Monster*)

It is a major breakthrough that today few reputable scientists will
boldly declare that the beast does *not* exist; whereas in the past, few
reputable scientists would declare openly that the beast *did* exist. This
is still not to say that naturalists, zoologists, and biologists are actively
planning to investigate the mystery; they are not. But they are in the
process of changing their official minds, and that takes a while.

In attempting to refute the evidence scientists have ignored certain
aspects and distorted others, as have some monster-hunters in advocating the evidence. But the skeptics' most amusing line of reasoning
in denying the beast's existence is the so-called "negative evidence"
argument. Many scientists argue that the beast does not exist because
of the "negative evidence" against it, including the absence of bones
or carcasses. It's an argument that smacks of *Alice in Wonderland*. One
can see hosts of scientists gathering "negative evidence," sitting stiffly
at long tables making lists of things they've never found, which proves
they don't exist. (As for myself, I've never seen Pittsburgh.) Of course,
there's no such thing as negative evidence. One cannot offer the ab-

sence of something as a positive piece of data. One can only deal with positive evidence positively, and there is reliable positive evidence for the beast.

Like all of us, scientists are timid about endangering their livelihoods, regardless of their professed dedication to "truth." They believe—and may be right—that actively advocating research projects at Loch Ness would damage their careers. Science is far more than test tubes and instruments. It also includes in its framework the attitudes, prejudices, blind spots, and intuitions of its practitioners.

The conclusion that the beast exists seems unavoidable from the evidence, but gleaning from that evidence exactly what sort of an animal swims beneath the loch is another story. Monster-hunters delight in sifting through the data, speculating, picking a fact here, a sighting there, a zoological theory everywhere, and building a castle-in-the-air case for one sort of animal or another.

All their cases are, however, very shaky constructions, for each case has valid scientific arguments against it, even considering science's ignorance of the unknown animals Nature could have constructed in her countless evolutionary experiments.

But the sketchiness of the evidence doesn't matter to monster-hunters. Each one—save a few—has a little conceptual beastie in his head, swimming about, living and breathing. Peter Costello, author of *In Search of Lake Monsters*, for instance, opts for a long-necked seal as his favorite candidate for the Loch Ness monster. It is a tempting theory; witnesses who have seen the beast on land say it lopes about like a seal, and the flippers are reminiscent of a seal's. But there are problems. The animal is seldom seen above water or on land—very unseallike behavior. And nobody has ever captured a long-necked seal; unusual for such curious, friendly creatures as seals.

F. W. Holiday, a monster-hunter and fishing writer—perhaps predictably—likes worms. Author of the *Great Orm of Loch Ness*, he argues tirelessly that the beast is a huge worm or slug. Holiday glosses over the reptilian or mammalian characteristics of the beast in his search for wormness. For one thing, the swimming motions of the animal, its solid humps, and its excursions on land all suggest a sturdy skeleton. Holiday has waxed ecstatic over the discovery near Chicago of a fossilized long-necked, round-bodied worm known as the Tully monster, and he advances this creature as a possible forerunner of the "orm." However, the reader of his book soon discovers that this creature is only about a foot long. Such a leap from inches to yards must be a strain even for a beast as great as the one in the loch.

But surely science can do better. Dr. Roy Mackal has gathered the sightings, photographs, and sonar evidence in *The Monsters of Loch Ness, and* has proceeded to dissect them meticulously. The results are often like dissecting warm Jell-O. It isn't easy to extract good, hard data from witnesses who at the time of their sightings were in the process of being frightened half to death; or from pictures that look as if they've been taken through gauze. But Mackal does the best he can, using the evidence to construct a table of 32 of the beast's characteristics (color, size, appendages, skin texture, etc.) and comparing the monster-candidates according to how well they fit those characteristics. Dr. Mackal, college professor that he is, then gives each of the candidates a grade, by tallying up the percentage of characteristics that each known animal species has in common with the beast in the loch.

These are the scores he arrived at:

> *Sirenia* (sea cows, etc.) 47 percent
> *Pinnepedia* (sea lions, etc.) 57 percent
> Gastropods (snails) 59 percent
> *Plesiosauria,* 69 percent
> Anguiliformes (eels) 78 percent
> *Urodela Embolomeri* (amphibians such as newts and salamanders)
>   88 percent

So, there you have it; the professor votes for the amphibian, giving it a "B+." There are, of course, drawbacks to his theory. Not only must this amphibian have survived 250 million years to be the beast in the loch, but it must have never been found in any fossil formations, for Dr. Mackal has invented a new animal.

There is no need to invent a new animal to explain the beast. As many have said, the beast in the loch has a remarkable resemblance to a plesiosaur, a long-necked, flippered reptile that hunted fish in ancient seas. One particular type of plesiosaur, the elasmosaur, is the best candidate of the lot. The elasmosaur, with its extremely long neck, containing 76 vertebrae, and its broad, flat, inflexible trunk has been described as looking like a snake pulled through the body of a turtle. It flourished during the Cretaceous Period from 135 million to 65 million years ago, apparently dying out in the mysterious cataclysm that abruptly ended the golden age of the dinosaurs.

At 40 feet, the elasmosaur was the right length to be the beast in the loch. And, as with the beast in the loch, it propelled itself with powerful strokes of its large flippers, its round body and stubby tail being of little use in swimming. Although many plesiosaurs had long lizard-like heads, the elasmosaur possessed a smaller, rounder head as the beast is said to have. The elasmosaur fed on fish, whipping its long neck through the water to snare its prey. The beast in the loch has been seen to behave similarly. Many have reported sighting the hump of the beast, floating motionless in the water, suddenly dashing off and submerging, as if the animal were making a quick lunge to snare a fish.

Despite the remarkable similarities between the beast in the loch and the elasmosaur, there are "minor" difficulties. For one thing, an elasmosaur-beast would have had to survive without detection during centuries of human exploration of the oceans, no mean feat for an air-breathing creature. Also, paleontologists have pointed out that skeletal remains of plesiosaurs indicate that they could not raise their flippers above the level of their shoulders. This means that they were probably poor divers, spending most of their time paddling about on the surface of ancient seas—very unlike the beast in the loch, which is seldom seen on the surface. And, finally, plesiosaurs were warm-water creatures, presumably unable to regulate their internal temperature to adapt to the frigid waters found in Loch Ness.

Normally, skeptical scientists might be expected to scoff at the possibility of a creature thought to be extinct surviving from ages past. However, this put-down has been spoiled by a supposedly extinct fish called the coelacanth, which was discovered in 1938, living in the Indian Ocean. The five-foot-long coelacanth, an ugly brute of a fish, was the early ancestor of the amphibians which later crawled out onto land to colonize this new environment for animal life. Ironically, the earliest fossils of this survivor from the age of amphibians, are found in Scotland, Norway and Canada—which were squeezed together into one continent when the periodic droughts 370 million years ago spurred the fish to evolve the ability to live on land. Interestingly, the fossil record of the coelacanth stopped abruptly about 70 million years ago, when the animals migrated to the deep oceans.

If the beast in the loch is a prehistoric, deep-ocean creature, would it also have failed to leave fossils? Perhaps the paleontologists' argument that "no fossils mean no surviving prehistoric beast" is merely another example of negative evidence. Many monster-hunters would think so.

As for this writer, he is above all this speculation. He is not one of those annoying people who leaf to the back of a murder mystery to see who committed the crime. He is content to wait until the mystery is solved and to observe simply that, while the beast may look much like a plesiosaur, it may have evolved into that form in what biologists call convergent evolution. For example, whales have evolved to resemble fish because the streamlined shape and fins are the best adaptations to a life in the ocean. But whales are emphatically not fish.

But, gee, the beast really *does* look like an elasmosaur

🌐 Chapter Seven
THE CONTACTS

Doc sat on a box on the edge of the pier, staring intently at the paper sonar chart reeling out of the recorder. The cable from the recorder ran to the end of the pier, and over the side to a submerged sonar transducer, pulsing out into the brown waters.

It was a beautiful sunny morning, June 20, 1976, a perfect day to begin a new phase of the expedition. The underwater cameras had not yielded any results, so Doc had set up his sonar to scan the area around the camera to see if anything large was swimming by. Such a wider field of view would be useful to warn the camera operator of an impending contact, and also to give solid evidence for the large creatures.

Doc babied the machine, constantly jiggling its switches, poking its printed circuit cards and fiddling with its paper. The machine was old but serviceable, and Doc didn't discard things simply because they were old. He also owned an ancient strobe light for his camera, held together with tape and hope, that he refused to give up despite pleas from the manufacturer. After all, Doc was the inventor of the strobe light, the manufacturer felt, and he should set a good example. The company managers were constantly trying to get him to accept a new unit, but Doc remained attached to his old flashing friend.

The sonar worked beautifully in the loch. Doc could easily pick out the straight sonar trace marking the stationary underwater cameras. Then a delightful occurrence. Suddenly slashing across the paper were two large parallel traces like curved brush marks, perhaps two large fish swimming in from the bay, passing near the cameras. It was a good omen. Life was beginning to stir around the cameras. Perhaps Doc became a bit nervous sitting there alone, next to the deep loch, with large traces appearing on the machine. It was a good test, though, and soon Doc would lower his large side-scan towfish into the loch, and its longer cable would allow him to move the recorder into the control hut.

There was not the hurry or excitement about setting up the sonar that had marked the early part of the expedition. As the technological side of the expedition had taken a back seat, the human side had climbed into the front; the last days of June would see more of the human foibles of the expedition, and fewer from the loch.

The next day was a prime example. It began with a press conference, a low-key affair with a few reporters sitting and chatting with Charlie and John Lothrop in the Drumnadrochit Hotel bar. Since the beginning of the expedition, the press conferences had wound down from room-filling affairs, to back-room affairs attended by a few hardy reporters in search of a back-page filler. The press had become bored with the nuts and bolts of an expedition with nothing sensational to report. More and more of the "reporters" that showed up at the site were writers for publications such as business magazines that wouldn't be caught dead writing about Loch Ness. But the writers, on vacations with their families, were fascinated by the topic—and who could blame them?

There were also visiting scientists, and, of course, our single expedition groupie! Her husband, a well-to-do New York businessman had telephoned a week earlier, offering to donate a substantial amount of money to the research effort if only his wife could come to the loch and watch us work. We were sure that this lady, whose fascination with the beast had driven her husband to the offer, would be a rich, slightly screwy old dame, perhaps with a big feather hat and an Insta-matic. In any case, we declined the offer, joking to ourselves that the gentleman might well be packing the old lady off to Scotland while he fooled around a bit at home. But she decided to come anyway, and who should show up at the pier, but a charming, effervescent, intelligent red-headed young lady named Janet, who brightened the research site for a few days before moving on. So much for the "fooling around" theory. Of course, the contract with *The Times* had made everybody jumpy and suspicious. Charlie was convinced that Janet was a spy for

Time magazine, toward which some of the group had felt animosity since the magazine's rejection of the 1975 pictures. Janet minded the suspicion not in the least, peppering Doc with questions about sonar, and writing postcards amongst the camera equipment. Some groupie!

The Times reporters who had accompanied the expedition had not helped allay the suspicion about the press. Throughout the expedition, Wilford and Hosefros had assumed something of the nervous attitude of a mother hen with too many chicks. *The Times* contract with the expedition members had specified that they were to be given 24 hours' head start on any breaking news. The reporters were constantly worried that one of their expedition "chicks" would scurry out from under their protective wing and go chirping off to be heard by other reporters. John Wilford was subtle about his anxiety. With a gray-flecked beard and a dignified demeanor, he was one of those rare individuals who could probably retain his composure while in the process of falling down an open manhole. But the Loch Ness business was a strain even for him. He was charged, not only with writing about the expedition, but also with protecting *The Times'* interests. It was a tough proposition, considering that *The Times* was thousands of miles away and that nobody was quite sure what its interests were anyway. The sight of Charlie talking to a reporter, or of an approaching television film crew would produce in the apprehensive Wilford, a subtle widening of the eyes and a grim, worried smile.

Paul Hosefros was not subtle. The young red-headed photographer was new to being a *Times* photographer on an important assignment, and was full of the business of issuing directions, requests and requirements in the paper's name. Hosefros favored drastic measures such as confiscating "unauthorized" film taken of the expedition. Their last day at the loch—June 21, 1976—was not a pleasant one for them or many of the expedition members.

First, there had been a frustrating day on the loch with the sonar team. Finkelstein had previously detected a large object on the bottom —perhaps even a skeleton—and he was to dive that day to inspect it. The story of the dive would be a fine ending for Wilford's stay at the loch, regardless of the outcome, and the photographs would look good in *The Times*; so the engineers and the two reporters boarded the *Malaran* and steamed off down the loch for the day's adventure. And they steamed and steamed and *steamed* back and forth across the area in a fruitless search. Finkelstein could not detect the object again on the sonar, and it was a disgruntled *Times* team who headed for the dock that afternoon.

Back at the site, a group of the press had requested to be able to get close-up shots of the camerawork, angles already published by the *Times*. It was an assorted group, including Janet, our groupie, "Doonesbury" cartoonist Garry Trudeau, a CBS radio man, and a local news photographer.

They were bobbing up and down photographing Charlie ministering to Old Faithful, when suddenly, bearing down upon them was the *Malaran*, a red-headed, red-faced Hosefros posed George Washington-like on the bow shouting and waving his arms.

The large cruiser circled the group huddled in the rowboat, with Hosefros berating them. "What are you doing there? Who said you could do that?" *The Times'* maternal instincts erupted. Wilford and Hosefros left the docked *Malaran* and hurried to the local bar, finding the press officer—me—soothing his shot nerves with a glass of the rich local beer. His nerves were abruptly reshot as Wilford and Hosefros moved in, Wilford with eyes widened, grim smile set; Hosefros waving and shouting!

"What do you mean letting those people near the boats! Those are close-up pictures! They could have as good pictures as we have! We paid $20,000 for this expedition! The CBS radio guy is probably a spy for the television side!" The argument finally subsided more from exhaustion than from resolution, much to the disappointment of the local crowd in the bar, who had enjoyed the peculiar Americans immensely. *The Times* left as planned early the next day, but Wilford was tired, disillusioned; he had a vague feeling that the expedition had been poorly planned and poorly executed.

The pressure for results on the expedition members, although not overt, had been mounting. Wilford had authored as many reports of preparations, and as many "mood" articles about the loch as he could logically write, and Hosefros had taken all the pictures he could ever want of cameras being dunked in the water. The NBC crew had filmed all the interviews, monitoring, meetings and camera-splashings they would ever need. All the other journalists visiting the research site seemed to be pushing for some dramatic climax, whether it be the triumphant discovery of the beast, or a dismal admission of failure. An ambiguous situation did not make good copy, and was certainly not the stuff of exciting headlines.

It was high time for the beast to appear, and for some reason, the journalists were all staring expectantly at Rines and his colleagues. They seemed to believe that the monster-hunters and their technology possessed some power to call up the beast, rather than being, like everybody else, at the mercy of an unfathomable animal in an unfathomable loch. Rines and the others had always expressed buoyant optimism about their chances, but had never issued brash predictions. The press had tended to take their optimism for certainty.

Of course, it was silly to expect a thousand-year-old mystery to be solved in a single month, on-cue for radio, television and newspapers. But such was the expectation, nurtured no doubt by the modern Western tradition of neatly packaged adventure stories, nicely fitting a newspaper column or a TV time slot, complete with commercials.

The pressure for results was especially frustrating because always lurking about was vague, tantalizing evidence that the beast was out there in the loch somewhere, and it was just a matter of luck to get that one sensational photograph. For instance, on June 21, after the morning press conference, Charlie had glimpsed *something* on the loch. His sighting had been at just about the most opportune time possible— while he was taping a radio interview. Standing on the end of the stone pier with BBC announcer Stewart Robertson, Charlie was explaining for Robertson's tape recorder one of the expedition's pieces of equipment:

". . . it's a Questar telescope made over in New Hope, Pennsylvania, and, of course it's used for looking up at the stars," said Charlie. As he spoke he casually looked out over the loch.

"Over here we're using it to scan the surface of the waters of Loch Ness and, uhhh, incidentally I see something interesting in the water out there. I hope that isn't Nessie coming along right now, or we'll miss it if it is." Charlie stayed cool. Decades of training had taught him to remain calm no matter what. And his cool was catching, for the radio announcer stayed cool, calmly asking:

"That looks like a rock, doesn't it?"

"No, no. It was way out. It's gone now. It just disappeared."

"What do you think it was? I didn't see it," said Robertson.

"Well it could've been—I don't know what it was. It was something that came up and went down. It might have been a fish."

"Which is pretty unusual just now, isn't it?"

"Yes, it is, that's right. Uhh, there it is. See it? See it?" Charlie's voice rose ever so slightly. Stay cool. Observe. Take data. The black object rose ponderously about a quarter of a mile away and then submerged.

"Very interesting," said Charlie.

"It was a rather small object, wasn't it?"

"Yes, it was very small. What it is I don't know, but it was interesting."

It wasn't until Robertson got home and Charlie's cool-infection wore off that the reporter realized what he'd seen. He'd seen a small object above the surface, just for a second or two. Then he noticed a huge wake, and then it just disappeared. Fish don't make huge wakes and otters don't submerge and stay down. For the object to have been visible at one-quarter mile, it would have to have been at least some size.

In Charlie's words, "Very interesting."

So eager were we for results during the final days of June that we occasionally leaped to conclusions, landing with an embarrassing thud. The most heartbreaking episode occurred about 9:30 a.m. on June 23, 1976, as Rines was showing a group of Boy Scouts around the research site. He delighted in teaching youngsters; their eagerness to learn rewarded his enjoyment of teaching. Leading the group out to the edge of the dock, he was patiently explaining about each camera hung from the research boat. As usual, Doc was handing out the colored postcards of amazing flash pictures. He had brought a carton full of the postcards, and everyone he met got a couple. One showed a delicate crown of droplets splashed up when a drop of milk splashed into a still pool. The other was an instantaneous picture in midflight of a bullet that had just ripped through a bright red apple. ("That's how we make applesauce in America," Doc would tell the wide-eyed kids.) In the control hut, the crotchety sonar machine was working perfectly, and a slow, reel of paper showed the straight, steady line marking the reflection of the beam off the cameras. Lothrop had just seen some sort of trace on the machine and called Charlie in.

With a heart-stopping suddenness, a huge dark trace came edging ominously out of the recorder, moving toward the line marking the cameras. Charlie saw it and set Lothrop to work pressing the buttons to fire off the cameras as the trace approached them. Charlie leaped off the porch and ran for Rines, who was standing on the pier with the Scouts, not 100 feet from the underwater cameras. Finkelstein walked in, saw the trace, and immediately hurried out to see if there were boats in the area. The bubbles from oars and boat wakes could reflect the sonar beam and create false traces on the sonar. Pandemonium broke loose, with Lothrop firing the cameras, excited expedition members crowded around watching the huge trace, and Boy Scouts pressing at the windows. The boys were let in one by one to marvel at the trace and enjoy the excitement.

Then the trace was gone, but Lothrop had fired the cameras many times during the episode. Rines was ecstatic, taking me aside to brief be about contacting *The New York Times'* London office with the news.

"Tell them the sonar blip had the same dimensional extent in 1972," he said excitedly. "Tell them it had the same type of multiple trace echo, and the same type of approach to the camera from behind as in 1975. And, if you think you should, you can tell them it had the same bumping of the camera in 1975." As we had examined the sonar record, it seemed as if the straight line of the camera trace had deflected when the unknown trace touched it.

But something was not quite right about the trace. I had seen rowboats plowing about near the cameras before, and the bubbles in their wakes had created traces on the sonar because the transducer was so close to the surface of the water. Was this trace a boat, too? I began to gather statements from the various witnesses. Rines, on the dock with the Scouts, had seen no boat at the moment he was called in to see the trace coming off the machine. Finkelstein, a sonar expert, had checked the water the moment he had come in and had seen no boats. And Finkelstein said he had seen a "slick" around the camera boat, as if something large were just under the water. I had looked at the loch myself during the trace and had seen no other boat near the *Hunter*. The NBC camera crew was milking the episode for all it was worth, interviewing witnesses and filming the sonar trace. They were delighted with some action after all the waiting. But then came the odd little detail that would eventually nullify the discovery. During the excitement, Finkelstein had run down to see if all the boats were at the dock, and had found McGowan, sitting bright-eyed and bushy-bearded in a dinghy. McGowan said he had just arrived on shore in the dinghy from the *Malaran* and walked up to the hut when all the commotion had broken out.

We decided to see what sonar trace a boat in the loch would leave on the chart, and McGowan went out in a rowboat to retrace the

Malaran-to-shore path. As we watched the dark sonar trace come out of the machine, I realized what had happened that morning. The sonar recorder had been set to record very slowly, and the trace of McGowan's boat wake had not begun emerging from the slow-reacting machine until after the boat had passed—in fact, after it had already docked.

Several of us were certain the trace that had excited us had been just a wake from McGowan's boat, but the evidence was slow to sink in with some of the expedition members. The excitement had been so invigorating, the hopes so high, that it took them time to come down, especially for Rines. For him, the contact had been so *right*. At the right time, with the right witnesses, and the right characteristics. He let the doubts about the contact sink in, but very slowly. Predictably, the underwater photographs of the event showed nothing.

But the sonar traces which began showing up the next day—June 24, 1976—were a totally different case. We began to see an almost daily appearance in the narrow sonar beam of large solid objects, larger than fish. And this time the watchers knew to make sure no boats had been in the area for a good while. Doc's sonar fish pulsed a narrow, vertical fan-shaped beam out into the loch. Even though his sonar "eye" watching the cameras was narrow, and limited—about six feet wide at a 100-foot distance—it was seeing *something*. The sonar watch was not constant, but only as the expedition members could manage. Even so, they were greeted by target after target. There was something large out there—and it was moving!

On June 24, 1976, at 7:18, 8:52, and 8:56 A.M. came objects which presented about a six-foot-wide target to the beam. They stayed in the beam for only a few seconds and were gone. The traces of the objects far out in the bay looked like small brush-marks on the paper. The targets were, alas, also far away from the cameras.

On June 25 and 28, more large targets, again too far out for the cameras to photograph, and again several yards to target width. The large, mysterious traces were promising. At least Doc, Charlie, and Rines could see that something was there, but not approaching the cameras, rather than relying on instinct. We watched the machine hungrily, knowing that only a few hundred yards away was something large that we were just itching to photograph.

The group's attention was diverted briefly from the sonar by the arrival from the laboratory of a new batch of developed films. They were more of the cassettes from Old Faithful which was still clicking away steadily in the loch. By now Old Faithful had clicked off 34,000 frames into the loch, with only a few fish showing up on the frames. But it took only a few successes to make the mission, and one of these rolls might be the blockbuster. We were especially interested in the roll included in the latest batch, which had been in the camera the night Charlie had seen mysterious haze and shadows on the television screen.

Charlie set up the film projector in the control cottage's tiny bathroom which he had commandeered as a darkroom—sometimes much to the discomfort of expedition members. He sat on the toilet seat, threaded the film through the special elapsed-time projector on a board over the bathtub, and began to project the film frame by frame on a small sheet of paper on the wall. For hundreds of frames there was nothing but the brown loch water with peat particles reflecting in the strobe flash. Then abruptly, a thin veil seemed to dance its way up the screen as Charlie clicked off the frames. He went back and reran the film. Again a whitish veil in the dark waters. It was a line of demarcation of silt stirred from the bottom or perhaps carried into the quiet bay by an inflowing stream. It was disappointing. The mystery of Charlie's midnight encounter would remain, for all that Old Faithful captured was silt—but silt stirred up by what?

But at least the sonar was yielding results. The sonar traces of large objects continued to pop up during the last week in June, climaxing in two traces that were good evidence that a large animal swam under the loch, and that it was hesitating to approach the cameras. On June 30, 1976, at 10:44 P.M., Charlie's wife, Helen Wyckoff, was on sonar watch, fortunately having volunteered to begin a watch earlier than the usual midnight. She saw a trace from a large object, beginning gradually 120 yards from the camera as something came into the beam. The trace grew in size as the object moved steadily in toward the cameras. It slowed and stopped, hovering 80 yards from the camera. Was it watching the flash? Considering moving closer? It sat for a minute, presenting a target to the sonar beam about nine feet wide. Then it slowly moved away from the camera, stopping once for a moment before disappearing completely. As the object moved away, two small traces skittered across the sonar chart; perhaps fish disturbed by the movement. Helen called for Charlie who rushed in, saw the trace and headed immediately for the end of the pier to scan the waters. He could see the entire bay from where he stood, and miles of the main part of the loch. Nothing. The loch was flat calm. No boats, no ripples on the surface, no fish, fleeing the object. It was such a marvelous, flabbergasting idea that a human, sitting calmly and cozily onshore had watched waves of sound bouncing off a huge body, moving invisibly under the silent loch; a creature that could fascinate and frighten, only yards away under the water! Even though the engineers hadn't seen the beast or photographed it, they had touched it with their sound machine.

The trace seemed so animallike. One could almost feel a thought pattern in the pathway of the object. There was the movement in to investigate; the hovering; perhaps the watching; and then the decision to retreat, with a pause before slipping into the haven of deep water.

Charlie took over the watch at midnight and saw a few smaller targets far out in the bay. At 5:00 A.M., on July 1, 1976, he too was rewarded with the grand-daddy of all the traces—of a target 30 feet wide slashing through the sonar beam about 100 yards from the camera. It stayed in the beam about three minutes, producing a trace of parallel filaments before leaving. Again, another small trace had moved across the paper, quite probably a fish moving away from the object. Again Charlie rushed to the pier to be greeted only by the gray mists hovering over the still waters. The waters hid the huge beast well.

To Rines, the traces were triumphant confirmation that the animals still lived in the loch, but he was even more delighted by the fact that Doc and Charlie had written beside the traces *Nessiteras rhombopteryx*. They had become full-fledged monster-hunters.

Rines saw much of interest in the two most important 1976 sonar traces. The July 1 trace showed a number of parallel filaments totaling 30 feet in target width. It was as if the sonar beam was reflecting off a number of surfaces. This was similar to the parallel traces on Klein's 1970 sonar record, and a trace on the 1972 sonar contact with the large objects. There had also been another large object on the 1972 trace which gave a large solid trace, much like the June 30, 1975, sonar trace.

Rines squeezed the sonar evidence as hard as he could for significance. He believed that the parallel filaments were likely reflections from the animals' various parts when it presented itself head-on; reflections, for instance, from its head, front flippers, body, back flippers, etc. The more solid, smaller trace, Rines believed could be a side view of the animal.

Many of the expedition members had become convinced that the timid beast was put off by the unceasing activity of boats, people, and cars around the pier. They knew the expedition had become a major center of attention at the loch. Large motorboats would appear in the bay, anchoring, we believed, to watch us work. One careless yachtsman had tried to moor his boat to one of the camera buoys, and another had actually rammed the camera boat. The expedition site had also become a routine stop for the tour buses around the loch. One of the expedition members would be hard at work around the cottage and would hear a bus pull up on the road above the site He would look up and find a flock of blue-haired little old ladies, peering myopically down the hill at him, or taking photographs of the peculiar people looking for the monster. After a few moments of waiting with their cameras for the beast to show up, they would pile in the bus and tootle off to a ruined castle somewhere.

As July came in, even the sonar traces went out. The last traces, several yards wide, occurred on July 4. Monitoring of the sonar system continued, but no more traces were seen. Perhaps the disappearance had something to do with the installation of a large research barge to hold the cameras; perhaps not. But for the shore-based part of the expedition, it was time to turn to new experiments, new directions, and to build a better base for future operations. So much had been done, so much discovered about operating cameras in the loch. It would not be wasted.

✪ Chapter Eight
THE SCAN

Sonar proved to be the star of the 1976 expedition. The stationary
sonar beams had yielded to Doc and the other shore-based scientists
traces of large objects moving underwater. And the sonar search of
the loch bottom also provided the searchers with exciting discoveries.

Klein's side-scan sonar is certainly "elegant"—a word scientists be-
stow upon an especially clever mechanism or experiment. There is
elegance in the towfish's electronic arrangement to produce bursts
of sound into the water. Powered by batteries, the electronic circuit contains a capacitor which stores up a powerful charge of electricity, and then, when triggered, dumps the electricity into a crystal
transducer. The crystal rings with the electrical jolt, producing a
powerful sound pulse which courses out into the water. The returning
echoes from the bottom in turn ring the crystal—which now acts as a
receiver—changing the reflected sound back into electrical impulses.
These electrical pulses, containing information on how well the sound
has reflected off the bottom, are amplified in the towfish and sent up
the cable to the recorder on board the boat.

There is also elegance in how the sonar "sees" the bottom. Although
scientists can see hundreds of times farther underwater with sound
pulses than with light, there is a catch: sound cannot be focused into
an image with lenses as can light. So sound beams cannot be sprayed
about over the bottom as can light beams and focused into an image
after they've reflected off objects on the bottom. The sonar engineers

solved this problem by making each pulse of a sonar beam a narrow vertical blip of sound that examines only a thin slice of the ocean bottom and returns to the towfish with information only on that thin slice.

As the sonar towfish is pulled behind a boat, slice after slice of bottom is examined by the sonar beam. After each outward blip, the returning pulse streams back into the transducer, with the first echo coming back from the bottom nearest the towfish and each succeeding instant of echo reflecting from farther and farther away. The returning pulses are telling the towfish at each instant, "I have been heavily reflected off the bottom," or "I have been hardly reflected off the bottom." This heavy-hardly information is painted out on the sonar paper as a line. "Heavy" reflections produce a dark segment of line, "hardly" reflections produce a light segment. When the thin slices are painted out one after the other on the sonar paper, *voilà!* an image of the bottom is formed.

The recorder, another elegant contraption, has the job of painting out each thin slice of information on the recorder paper. Each time a sonar pulse is sent outward from the towfish toward the bottom, a tiny electrical contact on the recorder begins a thousandth-of-a-second race across the sonar paper, leaving a trail behind it on the paper. This tiny contact, on its superfast journey, receives the amplified electrical pulse of the sonar echo returning from the bottom. The electrical contact paints on the paper by means of an electrical reaction with a moist chemical on the paper, which turns dark when sparked with electrical energy.

If the thin slice of bottom contains a rock or other good sound reflector, the paper gets a heavy jolt of electricity from the contact; if there is sand or another poor sound reflector, a light jolt. A sonar scan down the loch is a rapid succession of lightning-fast pulses seeing slice after slice of the bottom, with the tiny electrical contact racing time after time across the sonar paper resulting in a picture with sound! Klein is rightfully proud of his ingenuity.

Klein's sonar had painted pictures of interesting objects on the loch bottom from the beginning of the sonar survey in June. Finkelstein was the first person to discover that the interesting sonar traces corresponded with interesting objects on the loch bottom. He was diving to inspect the object that he had, embarrassingly, not been able to relocate when *The Times* reporters were on board. Studying his sonar

Klein's sonar towfish emits a thin, vertical sheet of sound pulses from either side to scan the bottom, and a cone of sound pulses straight down to penetrate the bottom and reveal buried structures. (*Robert Ullrich*)

records of the earlier fruitless search, he discovered that the mysterious object had actually shown up on the sonar several times in their passes over the area. However, the boat approached the object from a different angle, and the sonar trace of the object appeared different on the sonar chart and went unrecognized by Finkelstein. It was a common occurrence with a sonar scan, in which reams of complex data streamed out of the recorder, requiring some time for the operator to hatch it in his mind.

So out went the *Malaran* again, and Finkelstein, McGowan, and Thomason easily rediscovered the object. The sonar trace of the object looked just as they would expect the regularly spaced rib bones of a large skeleton to look. The trace showed a series of small objects, laid out in a straight pattern a short distance apart, and extending for about 20 feet. Whatever is was, it was not a chance formation. And it was only about 35 feet down, a safe depth for diving.

Finkelstein donned his wetsuit and splashed into the loch, playing his flashlight around in the murk as he made for the bottom. He could see well enough, but there was still that worrisome gloom outside the small circle of his flashlight. He swam to the area of the trace and began sweeping the bottom with his light. After a few moments he came upon the mysterious formation. Rocks! The riblike formation was a straight line of rocks laid out on the bottom! Searching a bit farther, he discovered a small circle of rocks with burnt sticks in the middle. Very simple; somebody had merely built a campfire here. But wait a minute: how could someone build a campfire or a line of rocks 35 feet down in a cold murky loch? It could only have been built when the loch was much lower, and who knew when that had been!

Finkelstein was swimming easily along, playing his light over the bottom when, just ahead, barely illuminated by the beam, was a hump on the bottom. It was a two-foot-wide, 30-foot-long hump on an otherwise flat, sandy bottom.

"My eyes bugged out of my mask! Along the side of the formation were ripples that looked like ribs," Finkelstein said later. He approached the formation. He touched it; it was soft. He broke off a piece, which came off easily in his hands. It was a soft lump of clay. He surfaced excitedly and gave the sample of clay to McGowan, who soberly pronounced it clay.

The tight schedule of the survey prevented Finkelstein from going back to investigate the formation further. But the memory of the peculiar monster-shaped formation would stay with him. He found out later that there could, indeed, have been a skeleton in that formation, but that it might have collected silt around itself, or sunk into the ooze, leaving a riblike impression in the clay. He just didn't know.

The sonar search continued as steadily as did the land-based effort to photograph the beast. But the relationships among the sonar searchers were so different that the two efforts could well have been two separate expeditions.

Onshore, working with the underwater cameras and the stationary sonar beam were the old professionals. Wyckoff, Edgerton, Lothrop, and Rines were all experienced men and experts of such single-mindedness that they could bury disappointments and disputes beneath the weight of that single-mindedness. They all spoke the same language of photography, although different dialects. Doc knew flash strobes, Charlie knew films, Lothrop knew camera mechanisms, and Rines could speak a good smattering of each.

But the sonar team—Finkelstein, McGowan, Thomason, and later Klein—was a mismatched group, with each member knowing little of the other's specialty. Finkelstein was a whiz with sonar, but had been on few field trips and hadn't developed the sensitivity to other disciplines that he needed. McGowan was a pick-and-shovel paleontologist, inexperienced with the complex eccentricities of electronics and sonar, much less with an unpredictable loch. And Thomason was a young biologist who had yet to specialized.

The result was that the *Malaran* suffered internal personality storms, as well as those produced by the loch. McGowan had arrived at the loch two weeks before Finkelstein and had spent the time puttering about, getting himself into more and more of a stew about the lack of progress. When Finkelstein finally arrived, the sonar gear was held up in customs. The inspectors were trying to figure out, among other things, whether Finkelstein's diving underwear, which he shipped with the sonar gear, could logically be termed scientific equipment. Finkelstein also spent time after his arrival aiding the shore-based part of the expedition with his diving and electronics skills, which made McGowan stew even more.

Finally the sonar arrived, but needed considerable repair and adjustment, and McGowan exploded. "We've been sort of standing about on one foot with our thumbs up our bums waiting for Finkelstein to get started!" he complained.

Meanwhile, Finkelstein, the other side of the scientific Odd Couple, was becoming more and more exasperated at McGowan's lack of expertise in some of the basic skills needed for sonar exploration. McGowan piloted the boat haphazardly and had little respect for electronic gear—once standing on the $5,000 sonar towfish to reach over the side of the boat.

The battle was on, and the sonar team puttered and squabbled its way down the loch, with McGowan at the wheel, Finkelstein at the recorder, and Thomason caught in the middle.

"Now turn right," Finkelstein would order, monitoring the sonar recorder. "No! No, goddammit—don't stop turning right, keep on turning right. Jesus Christ!"

A fuming McGowan piloted the boat as best he could, determined to stay the captain of the boat and of the sonar search. They worked like a well-rusted machine. Finkelstein firmly believed that McGowan at the wheel had all the sense of a snail, and McGowan was just as convinced that Finkelstein at the sonar recorder had all the sensitivity of a fire hydrant.

Marty Klein was an experienced expeditioner, but even he was swamped by the personality storm when he finally arrived at the loch. He innocently proposed to the team that they do a little study of the geology of the bottom before resuming the search for bones.

"Take me home," growled McGowan in answer to the proposal, disappearing down the steps into the boat's cabin to sulk and read a book. In a final explosion, Finkelstein eventually threw McGowan off the boat altogether, and he went home to give sour magazine interviews about the amateurism of the expedition. But he remained undaunted in his belief in the existence of the beast. He said he had gone to the loch 95 percent certain of the animal's existence and had left 100 percent certain.

The feud was not unusual. Fights, arguments, and animosity are common to scientific expeditions, as any scientist knows. Each scientist on an expedition is usually convinced of the all-importance of his own research and is accustomed to communing only with test tubes and research reports, rather than a crowd of real live people. And tension mounts under the pressure to gather as much data as possible in the limited time of the expedition. There have been many expeditions in which otherwise peaceful scientists, racing with the clock and confronted with fellow egocentrics, have resorted to threats, sabotage, and even fisticuffs.

The squabbles among the sonar team members, however, didn't stop the data from rolling in. Even with its black cloud hovering overhead, the *Malaran* and its crew gathered some of the most exciting evidence of the 1976 expedition to the loch.

After Finkelstein's encounter with the mysterious hump on the bottom, the scientists were eager to explore the loch further. The team first made a run across the width of the loch, using the bottom-penetrating beam of the Klein sonar to pierce the sediments. The sonar revealed not only the flat, U-shaped cross section of the loch, but also layer upon layer of ancient sediments beneath the bottom. Years earlier, Rines had detected evidence that the steep sides of the loch had continued straight down beneath the sediments; which hinted that the bedrock of the bottom was actually V-shaped, and of the loch had continued straight down beneath the sediments, which clogging the "V" over the millennia. But these echoes from the extensions under the sediments could have been merely side-echoes, said Doc and Klein—caused by stray reflections of sound off the side of the loch, onto the bottom, and finally into the sonar receiver.

Klein's bottom-penetrating scan confirmed that Rines' extensions were not real at all, but merely side-echoes. Klein had picked up readings of other sediment layers beneath the bottom that Rines should have seen, too, if his sonar had penetrated deep enough into the sediments to pick up a real, extended wall of bedrock.

In their search for bones in the shallows, the team first had to overcome one minor problem: the loch had almost no shallows. The underwater dropoffs from shore were so precipitous that the *Malaran's* bow could be in the shallows while its stern floated over 100-foot depths. But after consulting old charts and doing some reconnoitering, the team finally found enough shallow areas to keep them busy.

Their first major search took place at Lochend, where the loch gradually slopes up to a sandy beach. Back and forth they towed the sonar fish, making one parallel search run after another to cover the area. Then they ran perpendicular paths to make sure they hadn't missed anything. As it inched out of the recorder, the recorder paper revealed a complex bottom strewn with odd objects and peculiar formations. The search would definitely not be a simple case of a magnificent carcass resting obviously on a featureless underwater desert. The sonar searchers would have to go over and over the paper to pull information out of the complex traces.

An odd circular formation slowly edged out of the recorder on one of the runs. George Reid, the surveyor aiding them, said that a huge steam engine had been in the water in the area. Perhaps the formation was that engine, so they named the trace "The Steam Engine" and went about their business. Other circular formations also printed out on the records, but the sonar team was so buried under data that they had little time to wonder about them. They heard various stories of underwater mines exploded in the area, and of dredging, and accepted that the circles could have been due to those activities.

They next turned their attention to the steep sides of the loch. In 1970 Klein had seen on his sonar what he thought were underwater caves under the loch, in which the beasts could hide. In 1976 Klein searched the loch even more thoroughly, running his sonar along miles of the sides. He found on both sides a remarkable geology of ridges and undercuts. For a second time he confirmed that there were indeed underwater lairs in which large beasts could hide.

Each evening after the sonar runs, the team members would lug to the control hut sonar records of a bottom teeming with interesting objects. There was an odd squarish underwater formation near Cherry Island, which is an ancient man-made island-fort in the loch. In another area there was a trace of what they believed to be a broken shipwreck.

They were surveying at the far ends of the loch, so it was ironic that they should discover one of the most fascinating underwater objects lying on the bottom near Temple Pier, within hailing distance of the expedition's base. Their run that day was to be just a quick tow past the pier to see if they could pick up the underwater cameras on the sonar. The cameras did show on the sonar chart, as well as the moorings of the various boats; and even a large wooden coal barge sunk off the pier decades ago. But something else came out of the sonar, quite near the coal barge. It was a slim object, about 20 or 30 feet long, resting on the bottom. There were peculiar protrusions from its sides. Finkelstein wanted badly to dive to investigate the target, but was told the area had been thoroughly investigated. But had it really? Nobody could tell him what the unknown object was. And what a delicious irony if the final answer to the mystery of the beast lay practically underneath the area where hundreds of monster-hunters had launched their ambitious expeditions. Diving took time and time was short, so the team pressed on, leaving another mystery for later.

One mystery, however, simply begged to be solved. The underwater circles they had seen on the earlier runs at Lochend still haunted the sonar team. Finally, on July 6, 1976, they gave in to their curiosity and set out in the *Malaran* to discover just what had created the intriguing ring formations on their sonar.

They reached the area, launched the towfish into the water, and began a run to detect the rings. Finally a ring showed itself on the recorder, and they launched a buoy to mark it. Turning the boat around and scanning back in the other direction, they found the ring again, and launched a second marker. But these locations were not precise enough for divers searching a murky loch. So the team ran a third scan between the two markers, setting a buoy more precisely when the ring again printed out on the sonar trace. Finkelstein and Sam Raymond dove first, making their way down the buoy rope. The buoy weight had landed almost dead on a tire dumped in the loch. The tire seemed to be amidst a pile of rocks, and in the murk, the pile appeared to be curved. The divers made their way around the curve, and discovered that the sonar had seen a gigantic circle constructed from thousands of rocks. Finkelstein shot to the surface, shouting to a puzzled Klein, "It's a ring of stones with a tire in the middle!" Raymond surfaced next, confirming that Finkelstein had not been merely hallucinating.

A jubilant Klein and Finkelstein set to work examining their sonar charts once more, and realized that they had uncovered a mother lode of stone circles—big ones and little ones; single circles and circles intertwined with others; circles laid out in a straight line and circles in no particular order.

They knew that the circles could only have been man-made and that they must have been built thousands of years ago when the loch was much lower. The sonar experts would have to return to America and spend time studying their records and the history of such circles to understand their full significance. But they knew then they were onto something big. It was a tradition in the sonar survey business to name sonar targets, so the team named the stone circles "Kleinhenge" and continued triumphantly on with their survey. Of all the expedition members, Klein and Finkelstein were undoubtedly gleaning the most satisfaction from their efforts, for Klein's sonar was unveiling a myriad of fascinating objects under the loch. By all rights his findings should attract scientists of all disciplines to the loch for further studies. Klein's sonar had added another dimension to the scientific adventure serial that was Loch Ness.

Of course with any serial, each episode must have a cliffhanger ending, leaving the viewer wondering what will happen next. The sonar recorder quite soon brought forth that cliffhanger. On one of their last sonar runs in Borlum Bay near Fort Augustus, in about 300 feet of water, the team picked up a 30-foot-long object resting on the loch bottom. Klein couldn't resist monsterlike descriptions. "The target has a carcasslike shape with necklike projections," he wrote later. "It does not look like any of the other targets which we picked up in the loch."

Always careful, Klein did make the disclaimer: "Of course, it would be wild speculation to make any assumptions about this target without further investigation." But his heart clearly wasn't in the disclaimer, and he remained intrigued by the object, naming it "The Average Plesiosaur." Klein's excitement also led the other expedition members to become interested—Klein was an expert with his sonar, having designed the first commercial side-scan ever manufactured. If *he* was excited, the target was certainly something to be excited about.

Toward the end of July 1976, the team ended their sonar search, but the discoveries had by no means ceased. Klein and Finkelstein flew back to their New Hampshire laboratory and spent the next months poring over the complex records. They spread the sonar charts on a large table in one room of their laboratory and examined them whenever they had the chance. It was a worthwhile pastime. One day while examining the charts, the perfect outline of an airplane suddenly revealed itself. The sonar had beautifully imaged a World War II airplane that had gone down in the loch in about 100 feet of water. The 65-foot PBY "Flying Boat" looked in good condition, and the sonar trace even outlined the twin engines.

Still later, Klein and Finkelstein made an even more startling discovery. They found an entirely separate set of stone rings in the loch, far deeper than the first. While the first set of stone rings rested in about 30 feet of water, the second set was at least 75 feet deep in the loch. There were two mammoth circles—apparently solid piles of rocks 100 feet and 50 feet in diameter. The circles were connected by a long row of "dots"—almost certainly rocks—about six feet in diameter. And surrounding the long row of dots were more dots arranged in a third circle about 150 feet in diameter. Klein speculated that the remarkable structure deep in the loch may have been some sort of calendar or giant clock, constructed by ancients, but only detailed study would tell. He revised his names, calling the shallow set of rings Kleinhenge I, and the deeper set Kleinhenge II.

Klein's findings had raised a mass of questions for other scientists to answer. The different levels of Kleinhenge I and Kleinhenge II quite likely meant that they had been built at different periods, on the existing "beach" at their respective times. This would present geologists a fascinating puzzle of the history of water levels in the loch after it had been freed of the glaciers that filled the Great Glen thousands of years ago.

The primary mystery was the rings themselves. There are over 900 such stone rings throughout the British Isles, including the Loch Ness area. They were built by prehistoric settlers during a period from 4,500 to 3,000 years ago. The rings—the most popular of which is Stonehenge—are remarkable feats of construction for such primitive peoples. Some of the circles required the transportation of thousands of rocks, about a foot in diameter to the site, to be piled in massive rings. Other rings feature huge upright stones weighing thousands of pounds, arranged in precise circles. Associated with such stone ring structures may be extensive banks, ditches, single stones, avenues of stones, or other auxiliary constructions. The centers of the circles were often burial sites for cremated bones, which were piled in the dark chambers to be withdrawn for ceremonies. White stones, collections of broken pottery, fertile earth, tools, and other magical offerings have been found amidst the circles by archaeologists.

The megalithic monuments may have been used as religious centers for appeasing the gods of the ancients, or the powerful forces of nature that ruled their lives. The circles were, perhaps astronomical calculators, or even prehistoric town halls. But the circles remain mysterious, for over the millennia they have been plundered, moved, and destroyed, spoiling the chance for careful archaeological studies that may have revealed the reasons such primitive ancients were moved to such powerful labors. As Aubrey Burl, an expert on the circles has said, "Today, like the dead fingers of time, the stones jut from the ground, stark and unyielding to the enquiries of men who for centuries have asked why stone circles were built."

Klein had discovered a wealth of circles possibly preserved from destruction for millennia beneath the loch. Perhaps they could speak of their origins to archaeologists.

⊛ Chapter Nine
THE EXPERIMENTS

The final month of the expedition was one of consolidation—of perfecting old methods and trying out new ones. The unprecedented drought in Europe had lowered the loch, which the monster-hunters believed prevented salmon from swimming in from the sea to spawn. There was no doubt that few fish were in the loch. By the end of the expedition, Charlie would have examined over 98,000 pictures taken by Old Faithful banging away in the bay over a two-month period. Of these, only 33 frames showed pictures of fish. In comparison, about a dozen fish and eels had shown on a single 2,000-frame roll of film the year before. The beast had little reason to move into the shallow waters to hunt, with no fish congregation in the bay.

Charlie had conjured another intriguing theory for the lack of results. Some monster-hunters theorized that the beast preferred cold waters and didn't surface because of the warm surface waters. Thus, an extensive surface layer of sun-warmed waters would drive the beast down into the cool depths. Charlie had taken temperature readings and discovered that the loch in the summer of 1976 was at a temperature of 57° Fahrenheit at least to a depth of 20 feet; in contrast to its usual uniform temperature of 42°. During the drought, the cold mountain streams feeding the loch had slowed to a trickle; without the influx of cooling mountain water, the still brown waters of the loch warmed under the summer sun's rays.

For whatever reasons, perhaps the beast would not yield its secrets

147

this year, or the next, or the next. The expedition members weren't worried, though. They were already looking ahead to a long period of sustained effort. They were as sure as ever that underwater photography was the way to success. There would be no more patient surface watches, waiting for the beast to poke its head up. Now scientists would follow it underwater to its natural habitat.

There was an air of permanence in new research installations at Temple Pier. A large, sturdy research raft, 16 feet by 20 feet, constructed out of steel barrels and wood, was moored in place of the research boat *Hunter*, which had been an awkward craft from which to hang cameras. Winches on the raft allowed the cameras to be cranked up easily, and the large, rigid raft allowed all the equipment to be aimed precisely. A permanent control hut, with plenty of work room for future projects, had been moved onto the pier.

The contingent of researchers at the loch was steadily growing. The National Geographic Society had sent its best underwater photographers, Emory Kristoff and David Doubilet, to the loch, along with sonar-activated underwater gear to hunt the beast, literally alongside Rines. They arrived with a large trawler, and placed their equipment just down from the pier. They were using bait such as kipper and even pulsing sound tones which they knew attracted sharks out into the loch. Perhaps the sounds would lure the beast too.

Rines and the expedition members were also developing more basic information about what their equipment could do under the loch. Ike Blonder had arrived and set the videotape recorder back into full operation, even solving the electrical interference problems in the system. Now the TV/stereo system was poised and ready, should the beast begin haunting the bay again.

Charlie had also begun precise studies of the limitations and possibilities of photography under the loch. He tested the television system by dangling a large white plastic basket at various distances in front of the camera, and had discovered the system to be far more sensitive than he had thought. With the right lighting, he could see an unheard-of 40 feet in the brown loch water. He had also measured the clarity of samples of loch water and now knew exactly what numbers to feed into his photographic equations.

Charlie was bubbling with plans for new camera setups featuring huge strobe lights aimed out into the loch from the research raft. In this future arrangement, Old Faithful and the other cameras would hang in the loch, attached to the automated sonar system. If the creature swam into the beam, it would be inundated by a flood of light from the strobes.

Charlie's increasing confidence about photography in the loch was heartening. Like the rest of the expedition members, he had been worried about the unknown; but for him it had been a purely technical unknown of light penetration, strobe lights, and cameras. But with this new information he could push the loch even harder with his cameras until it gave in to his probings.

The waning days of the expedition also saw a series of forays to take the camera to the beast, if the beast would not come to the camera. The portable camera rig engineered by Lothrop was taken to the area off Invermoriston and lowered into the water, watched over by a sonar beam aimed straight down, and listened to with an underwater hydrophone. Rines and others had spent three nights in late July waiting silently in the boats for something to approach. One night, the experiment almost paid off.

It was 3:00 A.M. on July 18, 1976, and many of the crew on the *Malaran* had nodded off, either on deck or below. Tim Dinsdale was lying on the deck, the hydrophone headphones on, asleep. Rines was nodding over the sonar recorder which steadily reeled out paper, showing the straight line marking the camera rig 30 feet below the boat. Suddenly, another blank trace began to etch out on the recorder, above the camera equipment. Dinsdale came abruptly to life at the same time exclaiming that he had heard a chirping noise on his earphones. There was a mad scramble to get a tape recorder going, but before they could set up the gear, the trace was gone. There were other sonar contacts in the several night watches, but none so exciting. It was another fascinating piece of evidence for Rines, but for others there were doubts. Wyckoff had been on board for one contact; he had seen nothing when he peered into the water at a time when the beast was supposed to be a mere five feet below the boat. Klein had examined the sonar trace of a contact with a large object and was mystified that the trace had remained always at the same depth, never seeming to gain or lose depth. An animal, Klein thought, would have swooped up or down. The evidence of the encounter was as murky as the loch.

In a hunt for an unknown quarry, one had to try every possible hunting technique no matter how offbeat, and July was a time for experiments at the fringes of possibility. Blonder and Rines conducted one experiment at setting up an electric field in the water to attract the creature. Oceanographers in Florida had discovered that fresh-water fish were lured by such fields, congregating around the positive electrodes of an underwater electrical field. One night on the *Malaran*, Rines and Blonder attached the positive electrode of a battery to the camera rig, and made a negative electrode from some wire mesh. Lowering the electrified apparatus over the side, they saw that their setup appeared to lure some small fish; but the results were inconclusive.

George Newton, the scientist from M.I.T., tested his sophisticated infrared scanner at the loch in July. He wanted to see whether it would work as an automatic beast detector by sensing the warmth of the beast's rising to the surface to breathe. Newton wasn't out to find the beast on this first foray to the loch. He wanted merely to discover whether the infrared scanner could detect warm objects on the loch surface. It was possible that the mists and rains could spoil the infrared detection, and the detector might be "blinded" by scattered rays from the sun or other heat sources. The borrowed infrared scanner, originally developed and used for the army, consisted of a hand-held scanner aimed at the area to be studied, and a small television screen which would show the "heat picture" produced by the object.

Of course, to test a device to search for warm objects, you need a warm object, so Newton built an electrically heated metal target to float across the loch in front of his scanner. His warm target consisted of an aluminum plate, heated to a precise temperature, and a plastic water tank, which would be at a precise temperature difference from the plate. When the plate and the water tank were mounted together on a raft and towed across the loch, Newton could use the scanner to detect the tiny temperature difference between them. He could tell precisely how small a temperature difference the instrument could see.

With his equipment mounted on the top of Urquhart Castle, Newton studied the images from the scanner as the test target crossed the bay. He discovered that the scanner was an excellent penetrator of the mists of the loch and could scan the waters for miles at night, when the human eye was useless. However, he discovered that frequent rains and the powerful rays of the midday sun would spoil infrared vision. Newton's infrared eye could be used in the loch, but it would be a back-burner project. The infrared system could detect nothing beneath the surface, and its long-range, blurry images would do little to identify the beast. What's more it was a terribly expensive eye—a basic infrared system would begin at $30,000. Nevertheless, Newton had studied the possibility carefully. In a search for an unknown beast, one had to try everything.

Rines and McGowan spent part of the last month at the loch developing methods to dredge the bottom for bones. Rines was intrigued by the possibility that animals which died on the steep sides of the loch might slip down into the border between the side and the flat bottom. He and McGowan set out in the *Malaran* to see if they could use sonar to guide a dredge along the border. Watching the sonar soundings of the loch's depths, they worked the *Malaran* along near the shore, scooping up samples of the ooze below. When the sonar began to register a sharp rise in the bottom, they backed the boat away from shore, for they knew they had passed the point where animal remains might have slipped down to the bottom. Rines and McGowan found no animal bones in their tests, but did dredge up a hot-water bottle, a lady's shoe, and considerable length of winch cable. Apparently, besides being the lair of a great unknown beast, and the guardian of monuments of an ancient civilization, Loch Ness was also an active trash dump.

With the end of July 1976, the scientific team tiredly trickled back to the United States, pensive at having to leave the beautiful loch behind. But there was still optimism, for they left a perfected set of gear for future hunts and a permanent base of operations, with a control hut and an instrument barge that would most certainly see years of further exploration.

They also left behind Old Faithful, hanging silently in the loch, waiting. The camera seemed to be a thematic thread weaving through all the adventures at the loch. It had seen the beast in 1972 and in 1975. Now it would be the source of a continuing hope for further results. Rines and Wyckoff had rigged the camera with the automated sonar trigger that would keep watch for several more months, waiting for a large object to swim into its sonar beam. Gordon MacKintosh, Tony Gerlings, and Alex Menzies, the owner of Temple Pier, had been taught to maintain the device, and the Scotsmen were delighted with the prospect of being in on the hunt. Charlie would return late in the fall to perform more camera experiments—perhaps some monitoring—and to batten down the equipment for the harsh winter. The next major expedition would feature exploration with underwater television and divers of Klein's carcasslike objects on the bottom. There would also be more sonar monitoring, better camera setups, and most importantly, a greater confidence that the engineers could use their technological power to obtain photographs and sonar traces of the beast. But the loch would be quiet until the monster-hunters regrouped, made further plans, and again attacked the mystery.

The monster-hunters had taken with them some of the loch's secrets. Charlie knew more about the brown waters and how to photograph in them. Klein had discovered his rings. Doc had obtained the remarkable sonar traces of large objects underwater. And Rines had developed a new bag of techniques to use in his future expeditions.

They also took with them the dead certainty that there *was* a Loch Ness monster. Any doubts had evaporated under the careful examinations of the past evidence, the talks with the reliable local citizens, and their own evidence.

Except for the sonar traces, the 1976 evidence for the animal was undoubtedly inadmissible scientifically. In fact, it was plain lousy. A glimpse of an object in the water or a shadow on the television screen wouldn't and shouldn't be accepted as valid proof of anything. But in any scientific controversy, the admissible evidence is merely the tip of the intellectual iceberg. Beneath the solid, tangible proof, there is always the huge mass of hints and indications, and even hunches, that support a theory. Doc's sonar traces had added to the visible tip of valid scientific evidence for the beast. And all our intriguing, exasperating, near-misses at the loch had added to the invisible, underlying mass of experiences that made the monster-hunters so confident of their quest. The beast was there.

⚛ Chapter Ten
THE LESSONS

The 1976 expedition was over, but it would blend into the next expedition and the one after that. With the 1976 effort, new technologies had been brought into play, and these, together with the earlier successes, made it certain that the search would continue.

Perhaps more important than any evidence was that the loch and its beast were becoming a subject for legitimate scientific inquiry. Zoologists had at least begun voicing support for the search, if not actually participating. The National Geographic Society had begun investigations at the loch, albeit timidly, and local government agencies and universities were contacting Rines to discuss their role in the studies. Seeing what technology had already accomplished at the loch, many high-technology companies were readily offering their products to be tried in the search. Telescopes, cameras, and other expensive equipment were being loaned or given.

The scientific community seemed to be gathering its courage to descend upon the loch in full force. It seemed as if the next underwater photograph of the beast—no matter how poor—would be all the excuse they needed. The evidence for the beast had never been the governing force behind scientific interest or disinterest before, and neither would it be in any new dawning of curiosity in the scientific community.

The controversy over the beast had been quite a trial for science, it was certain. The beast was a sharp blade thrust up into the scientific

153

arena for all scientists to teeter upon trying to maintain their intellectual balance. The wisest scientists balanced well upon the blade:

"Yes, there is legitimate evidence for the beast's existence, and it likely exists," they would proclaim teetering one way.

"No, there is far too little evidence to be sure of its existence, much less its identity," they would proclaim teetering the other.

But many scientists toppled off the blade. Either they ended up on the side of those who overanalyzed the sketchy data to proclaim that the beast was one animal or another. Or they fell off on the side of those who—damn the evidence—declared that the whole business was poppycock.

On the pro side was Sir Peter Scott, who had declared he thought the beast was a plesiosaur. And, of course there were the monster-hunters like Roy Mackal, who in his dissection of the evidence had soared far beyond the hard data. Mackal, for instance, in attempting to figure how many monsters the loch food supply could support, calculated the number of salmon in Loch Ness over the spawning period. His figure of 13 million adult salmon, or 19 billion juveniles astounded the fisheries experts. One wag declared, "This volume would so choke the lake even heretics could walk on the water."

But the most remarkable thing about Mackal's calculation, was that he had derived his whole mountain of numbers from a molehill-of-a-picture obtained from Rines. It was an underwater photograph of three salmon migrating into the River Enrick!

The con side of the monster controversy also had its share of silliness. Dr. Gordon Sheals, Keeper of Zoology at the British Museum of Natural History, had been a chief critic of the evidence for the beast, and in a BBC television program on the beast, marshaled his argument against its existence:

"Quite frankly, I think the whole idea is absolute nonsense," said Sheals. "In fact, I'm utterly confused and bewildered by the various arguments and ideas that have been put forth. But as I understand it, most of the believers now consider this wretched monster to be some sort of large, predatory reptile; some sort of plesiosaur. . . .

"And it's been suggested that these animals could be warm-blooded, although, of course, all living reptiles are cold-blooded, and therefore very much dependent upon the temperature of their surroundings. It's been suggested that they can retain their eggs within their bodies until they hatch, so in this way they could, perhaps, reproduce at great depths.

"Then again it's been suggested that they could be cannibals," Sheals continued. "This suggestion, of course, has been put forward to try to explain away the absence of any physical remains. And in a recent article I even saw the suggestion that they might have some sort of snorkel device.

"So it seems to me we should be quite clear about what we have been invited to accept—that in a relatively small body of water, in what is from a zoological viewpoint one of the best explored countries in the world, we have a population of large, predatory reptiles which *could* be warm-blooded, which *might* retain their eggs within their bodies until they hatch, and which *might* even be cannibals with snorkels. Now this I find very difficult to take," he concluded.

Very true. Anybody would find it difficult to take the large straw monster which Dr. Sheals set up, to triumphantly knock down. His magnificent hodgepodge of the various half-baked theories and speculations surrounding the beast were easy to refute. It is less easy to tackle the photographic, sonar, and eyewitness evidence, which Dr. Sheals does by adhering to the theory that "the thing we call the Loch Ness monster is really a mixture of many different things [which] could include rotting vegetable material, logs, tree stumps, tree roots, gases escaping from the bed of the loch, and commonplace objects which could be distorted by mirage effects."

At least Dr. Sheals had examined the evidence. The Loch Ness monster also attracted scientists who were quite willing to refute the beast's existence without resort to such niceties as considering the data. Adrian J. Desmond, British paleontologist and author of the popular book *The Hot-Blooded Dinosaurs*, was one such speculator. In letters to Sir Peter Scott released to the newspapers, he launched on a mathematical adventure to prove the absurdity of the idea of the Loch Ness monster. Beginning with estimates by oceanographers that the loch food supply could support up to 17 tons of monsters, and assuming that there were 30 monsters, he calculated that each monster would weigh about 1,100 pounds, a perfectly respectable and monstrous weight. However, contended Desmond, the reputed length of the beast is about 50 feet, which would make a 1,100-pound creature an emaciated lightweight. The basic figures on loch food supply and monster populations were, of course, shaky enough, but Desmond's assumptions about the creatures' average length had gone far beyond the bounds of even the sketchy known evidence. The huge majority of sightings had suggested a beast about half as long as the length Desmond picked. A 25-foot-long beast would have spoiled Desmond's adventure in speculative math.

Just as the beast in the loch brought out the theorizing "beast" in the scientists, so it revealed a few quirks in the journalism profession. The press had coined and popularized the term "Loch Ness monster" in the 1930s, and the concept was their toy. They showed the same sense of possessiveness and jealousy one might show over a favored toy. First of all, they refused to accept that the beast could be anything but a toy, to be brought out when news was slow and displayed for the amusement of readers. Thus, those such as Rines who would take the press's toy seriously must be either fools or charlatans. With this assumption, many journalists set out to gather evidence that could be used to prove Rines' foolishness or chicanery, merrily molding the results along the way.

Perhaps the most damaging such article to Rines' reputation and that of his 1975 pictures was the November 30, 1975, article in *The Sunday Times of London* by David Blundy. Amidst the early furor over the 1975 pictures, and their criticism by the British Museum of Natural History, Blundy's editor ordered Blundy in America to take a close look at Rines and his photographs. Blundy didn't interview Rines, but did interview Rines' brother-in-law Robert Needleman, Charlie Wyckoff, and a number of other people involved.

The result was a clever piece of journalism entitled "Nessie, This Is Your Best Show Yet," replete with the sarcasm reporters sometimes substitute for insight.

Rines, Needleman, Wyckoff and Edgerton were dubbed "a group of American lawyers" by Blundy, even though Needleman was the only one in the group who was strictly a lawyer.

Blundy judged the Academy of Applied Science as "less impressive in fact than its name suggests," without revealing his definition of "impressive," or from what information his judgment originated. Quotation marks were used like blunt instruments, as Blundy informed that the academy claims to have "300 members," the quotation marks insinuating that deception was a good possibility.

Blundy dismissed computer enhancement with a hoary joke that had made the rounds of the space centers when the technique was first developed to improve early photographs of Mars.

"People thought it was black magic. They'd say: 'What do you want to see, boys, mountains or craters?' " Blundy quoted a scientist as saying of computer enhancement.

The safest way to avoid facts that may spoil one's thesis is to omit them, so Blundy omitted the fact of Doc Edgerton's participation. Blundy informed his readers that in 1975 Rines "used two of Edgerton's 16–mm. flight research cameras," without specifying anywhere in the article who the mysterious "Edgerton" was.

Blundy was masterful, weaving out-of-context facts, and unattributed quotes into a whack at Rines. Of the 1975 photographs, he wrote, "To Rines, the result was that six frames out of the two thousand they took showed objects which could be interpreted as a 'prehistoric reptile.' "

Blundy thus ignored that even if the loch were infested with monsters, a camera snapping pictures every minute or so could easily use thousands upon thousands of pictures without capturing a picture of one. And who was the mysterious quoted person who had dubbed the pictures "prehistoric reptiles"? Rines had not.

As had so many reporters, Blundy raised greed as a motive for Rines' Loch Ness adventures. "Rines' own efforts to make money out of Nessie have so far met [little] success," he wrote. Blundy also quoted an impolitic statement of Needleman's that they hoped to make $100,000 from the pictures. Had Blundy investigated further, he would have discovered that Rines is already a comfortably wealthy man, and had designated any money from the pictures for research and conservation at Loch Ness, or scholarships for his law school. In fact, far from profiting from his Loch Ness research, Rines has poured considerable sums of his own money into the project.

After five paragraphs of quotes from scientists at the British Museum on photography—precisely the subject they knew nothing about —Blundy wound up his article by drawing on a technique many clever reporters use when their sources have dried up; they interview each other. His final quote was from John Durniak, picture editor of *Time*, who concluded of Rines and his colleagues: "They are a strange crew; either they don't understand publishing—or they don't want to."

Given that Blundy was not a science writer, and that the British press has a reputation for being rather cavalier with facts, perhaps the article was understandable. But the American press drew upon it, and upon other of the trumped-up British accounts for its own articles on Rines. *Science*, an otherwise eminently respectable scientific journal, ran a short piece in January 1976 on the scientific naming of the beast. The story contained the chestnut about how *Nessiteras rhombopteryx* was an anagram for "Monster hoax by Sir Peter S." The *Science* article also mentioned that a retired Scottish librarian had suggested that Rines' photo might show a fake movie monster lost in the loch. Of course, what *Science* failed to mention about the story was that the librarian hadn't even seen Rines' pictures when he made the statement and had relied on a general description of the photographs in the newspaper. (Since the initial charge, numerous people who have seen both the movie monster and the Rines photographs have said there is little resemblance between the two.)

If the press scoffed at Rines for taking their toy seriously, they became downright indignant when *The New York Times* took their toy away altogether by sponsoring the 1975 expedition on an exclusive basis. Disgruntled reporters began venting their ire on the expedition from the moment the *Times* arrangement was announced. There was, for example, a telephone call from a sour science writer for *The Wall Street Journal*, who announced that he would have no part in writing about the expedition under the conditions of *The Times* coverage. Other newspaper and magazine reporters gleefully searched for ways to twit *The Times* for its presumptuousness.

The *Columbia Journalism Review* certainly did its part, charging in its July/August 1976 issue that puffery had been committed by John Noble Wilford in the name of *The Times*. The *Review* article, entitled "Monster Swamps *Times*," accused *The Times* of failing to be skeptical, and then set out on its own tirade forgetting to be skeptical of its own sources. The writer, Jon Swan, accused *The Times* of failing to note the possible fakery and doubts surrounding Rines and the academy. Swan cited the tale of the Scottish librarian and the movie monster, as usual, failing to note that the librarian had not seen the pictures when he made his suggestion.

Swan accused *The Times* of failing to detail the past circus of absurd expeditions to the loch. He ignored the point that the 1976 expedition, with its high technology and its prominent participants, was a totally different situation. Swan managed to avoid mentioning Wyckoff,

Edgerton, or any of the other technologists whose mention might have foiled his anti-*Times* thesis.

Instead, Swan set up as his prize witness, one Andrew Rooney, a journalist who had written an "Op Ed" article on the subject which had been rejected by *The Times*. Swan said Rooney's rejected article contained some "potentially disconcerting revelations," among them a swipe at Rines' academic credentials. Swan quoted Rooney as saying of Rines, "He uses the title 'Doctor' on the strength of a degree he was given after a brief visit to Taiwan by National Chiao Tung University. It followed the gift of an electrical engineering research building to National Taiwan University by his father in 1969."

It was an odd slur from Rooney, who had interviewed Rines and had asked him about the degree, according to those present. Rines' "brief visit" to Taiwan had actually been many extensive visits over a period of several years during which he had consulted with the government, and delivered a series of published lectures. The thesis for his doctorate from National Chiao Tung University was a treatise on how to start high-technology companies in developing countries. The building was a surprise gift by several friends in honor of the senior Rines, given, in fact to a different university.

Another journalism magazine, *MORE* also came by Rooney's rejected article and published its own clever jibe at *The Times*, using the piece as ammunition. But *MORE* proved too clever for its own good. In its July/August 1976 report it first condemned *The Times'* reasons for rejecting the article, which were that it would require a lot of checking. But then, *MORE* proceeded to publish Rooney's allegations, apparently without checking them itself.

The press had obviously taken Rines and the beast for all the lampoon-value they could get out of them. While reporters claimed to be driven by their god Skepticism, they had forgotten its true meaning—suspended judgment or systematic doubt—and substituted one that fitted their mood—sarcasm. But in all the controversy caused by the press, the most damning accusation against them was that they had lost their sense of humor. The search for the Loch Ness monster, using new technological tools, was a fabulous, exciting adventure. If the beast did not exist, it would be a remarkable lesson in self-delusion; if the beast did exist, a triumph of independent thinking. Either way it was a glorious, fascinating story. Few critics of *The Times'* coverage of the expedition seemed to realize that *The Times* had devoted space and money to the story precisely because it was so much fun. Instead the critics grumbled into their typewriters while *Times* readers enjoyed Wilford's prose.

The press's heavy concentration on Rines' reputation was, to an extent, the correct editorial decision. Both before and after Rines' evidence was known in full, his reputation was a central issue in the controversy. Loch Ness had seen many hoaxes in the past, and many misinterpretations of evidence. However, the press's pursuit of Rines seemed to have had a punitive air about it. It recalled the reactions to new theories during the Middle Ages, when a heretical scientist, having hatched a revolutionary idea, was promptly clapped in irons and his religious faith called into question.

The press was not the only party in the inquisition. Scientists had also tended to examine Rines a little too minutely and his evidence a little too casually. For instance, the 1972 photographs and sonar evidence were quite persuasive, but they were ignored until the sensational-but-debatable 1975 photographs turned the public spotlight on Rines. Science had to be attracted by the pretty bauble of the 1975 photographs before noticing the solidity of the 1975 evidence.

In all the examinations of Rines, the only thing he can really be accused of in the end is a highly infectious enthusiasm. His doggedness in pursuing the beast and his eagerness in hammering home his evidence has attracted some of the most effective technologists in the world to his search.

But why such enthusiasm in the first place? The central human mystery in the expeditions was why Rines and the other monster-hunters, for that matter, would court frustration and spend their energies on such a seemingly frivolous quest.

True, all the expedition members had expressed perfectly logical reasons for coming to the loch. Rines wanted to teach science a lesson; Charlie wanted to solve a tough problem in photography; Doc wanted to instigate some people to flex their intellectual muscles; Klein wanted to try out his equipment and publicize his company; I wanted to record the adventure. But that was all only a clever front.

We all really wanted to go scaring off into the darkness, screaming and yelling like we did when we were kids, looking for the goblin. We wanted to prove to ourselves that amazing dragons could exist,

and that fairy tales could come true. It was a perfectly scientific attitude. As science-fiction writer Ray Bradbury once said, "The scientist
who isn't a child isn't a scientist."

As with all good scientists, we were in the process of trying to grow
up, to learn more about the dark places in our world. So many times
during the expedition we had heard one person or another lament
that we were dragging the fabulous myth of the beast out into the
open to deal it a deadly blow, to spoil their lovely visions of a magical
world where anything is possible. But they were wrong. We did want
to discover what made the beast tick, but only so we could open our
minds to the universe of other, even more fascinating questions about
the animal.

There was little danger that our search, even if totally successful,
would use up all the mystery about the beast. Most good scientists
know that science does little more than increase the sophistication
of our ignorance.

If we matured in our understanding of the beast, we would probably
enjoy the new mysteries even more. Ask any kid; grown-ups have all
the fun because they've graduated to all the toys that kids could never
play with. A jet airplane is far more fun than a paper glider; a trip to
the moon a far better adventure than a trip to grandma's. We just
wanted to grow up, to leave all those other ninnies behind with their
hazy dreams of dragons. We would see the dragon, learn about it,
find out where it came from, how it was made . . . and revel in the
explosion of new questions. That was science!

But even this powerful intellectual lure doesn't really explain the
personal lust of curiosity that attracts monster-hunters to the loch year
after year. The expedition had been far from successful in solving the
mystery of the beast. But it was enormously successful for me. I
finally came to understand the strange personal attraction the beast
holds for humans. On the 1976 expedition I was transformed into a
monster-hunter myself. The image of the beast evolved in my mind,
tantalizing and real, just as it had in the minds of countless others.

I had never been more than vaguely interested in the beast before.
I recall that in 1972 when I first read newspaper reports of the flipper
picture, I was slightly intrigued, but the information was filed quickly
away in my memory as of minor consequence. When the first reports
on the 1975 photographs began surfacing, they also created only a

mild itch of curiosity. At the time, becoming involved in publishing the photographs seemed a natural thing to do. I worked for a technological magazine, and Rines and the others had technological information to publish that would interest our readers. But the beast remained for me a creature of the intellect. The controversy over the evidence made the beast more of an irritant than a subject for fascination. I wondered whether all the fuss was worth it for such a speculative project.

But after coming to know Rines and his fellows, and hearing the logic of their evidence and seeing their confidence, there was little doubt that they were serious and sensible, and that they believed with all their souls in the beast they sought. Mild curiosity was replaced by strong interest—not just in the beast, but in the men who sought it and the other men who scoffed at them. I couldn't understand why they were so mesmerized by their quarry, so I offered to help them. Maybe I'd figure it out.

Then there was the magnificent loch; the concentration of the hunt; the disappointment of failure, but the fascination with the evidence that did appear. The fascination grew; it fed on the elusiveness of the beast, the exciting stories of people's encounters, and on the hard kernel of evidence that just wouldn't go away. The fascination exerted itself against those who were so mired in their convention that they couldn't examine the evidence dispassionately.

After the utter immersion in the effort and the concentration on the quarry, this huge, fantastic beast has now become for me an entrancing goal. Maybe seeing the animal, photographing it, and understanding it is one of those impossible tasks one sets just so he won't find himself fresh out of dreams. But I don't think so. In any case, I'm now an avowed monster-hunter. I want to go back to the loch again and again, to help in any way I can to discover more about the beast.

I dream about the beast now. I'll never forget my most vivid dream. I sit on the shore of the loch. It is twilight, and just offshore, I see an eruption of spray in the water. The water boils and seethes, and spouts of spray shoot into the air. There is something huge there in the middle, obscured by the spray. If only the spray would die down, I could see the object. There's definitely something there, but the damnable water keeps spewing about; the foam keeps boiling. I can't see clearly. . . .

Who knows? Maybe one day I'll find out what was in the midst of the watery upheaval in my dream. I'll be sitting there on the shore of the loch, and the beast will surface magnificently. I'll see a long muscular neck, an ugly head, a massive black hump swirling the waters.

Who knows? Maybe you'll be sitting beside me.

Urquhart Bay in Loch Ness. (*Robert Needleman*)

The most famous above-water photograph of what is likely the Loch Ness monster is the "surgeon's picture," taken by a London gynecologist on vacation in 1934. This photo is one of two, taken moments apart. The second shows the object leaning "forward" as it submerges. (*Wide World Photos*)

Robert Rines (left) and "Doc" Edgerton discuss the sonar contacts with the beast. (*Dennis Meredith*)

Charles Wyckoff prepares the TV/stereo camera rig for its first lowering. (*Dennis Meredith*)

Charles Wyckoff (left) and the author display the TV/stereo apparatus used in 1976. (Hosefros: *The New York Times*)

Charles Wyckoff and Robert Rines lower the large underwater camera rig into Loch Ness. (*Jeffrey Thomason*)

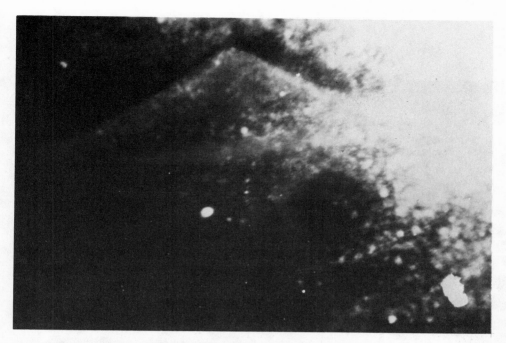

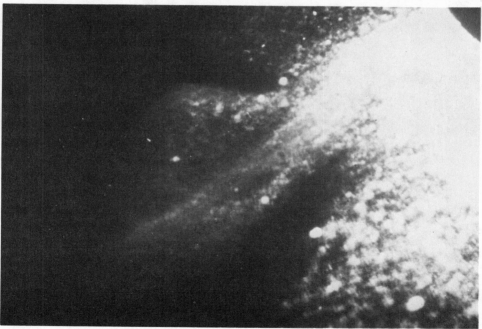

The first underwater pictures of the beast—the 1972 "flipper" pictures. The second was taken 45 seconds after the first, and both show an appendage about six feet long.
(*Academy of Applied Science*)

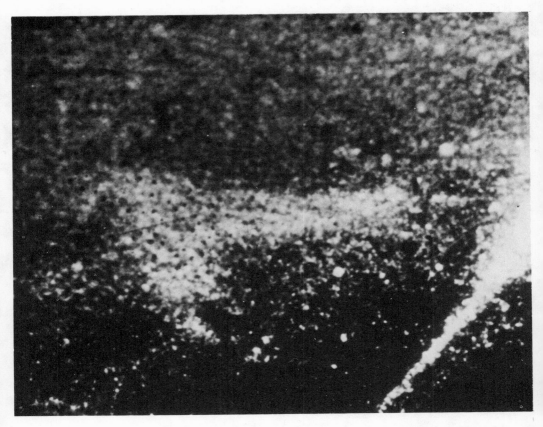

The 1972 "two-body" picture was taken when the sonar said there were two large objects in the sonar beam. (*Academy of Applied Science*)

The 1975 "body" shot of what appears to be the body, and head of a living creature. Two independent measurements yielded a length of about 20 feet. The dark square, lower left, is the film sprocket hole. (*Academy of Applied Science*)

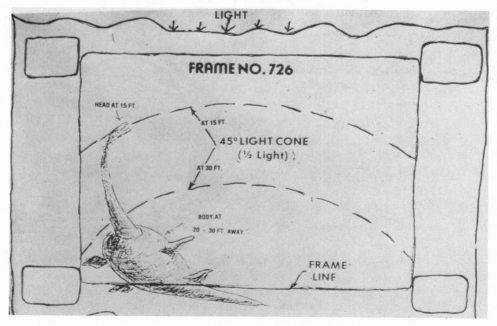

LIGHT

FRAME NO. 726

HEAD AT 15 FT.

AT 15 FT.

45° LIGHT CONE
(½ Light)

AT 30 FT.

BODY AT
20 - 30 FT. AWAY

FRAME
LINE

In analyzing the "body" shot, Charles Wyckoff sketched the position of the animal in the frame, showing where the beam of the strobe light hit the animal's body. (*Academy of Applied Science*)

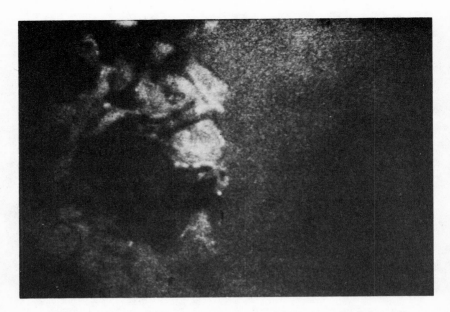

The 1975 "head" shot was obtained amidst a period of disturbance of the underwater camera in which it was bashed so hard it swung up to aim at the bottom of the boat from which it hung. The photograph is interpreted as being a horned head, showing "bilateral symmetry," with its mouth open toward the camera. (*Academy of Applied Science*)

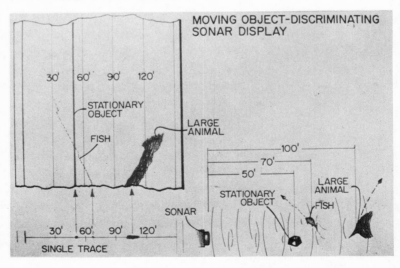

How to read a sonar chart from a stationary sonar. When the sonar beam bounces off an object underwater, the sonar recorder makes a mark on the chart, corresponding to the distance of the object from the sonar transducer. As the chart paper reels out of the recorder, the resulting trace is a record of how the object is moving in the beam from instant to instant. Stationary objects leave a straight-line trace on the recorder, because they never move. (*Academy of Applied Science*)

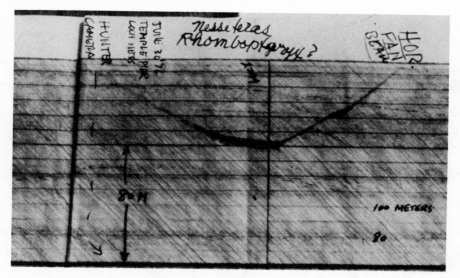

The June 30, 1976, sonar trace of a large, underwater object moving toward the cameras. As the sonar record reeled out of the recorder, left to right, the straight line at the bottom marked the reflection of the beam off the underwater cameras. The sonar record shows an object with a target width of about three meters. The object moved in toward the cameras, paused for about a minute, and then moved back out, pausing once before departing. Each horizontal marker line represents ten meters of distance from the sonar transducer. The small, thin traces are probably fish. (*Academy of Applied Science*)

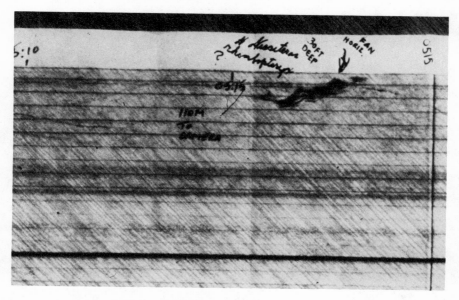

The July 1, 1976, sonar trace of a large object entering the sonar beam. The object has a target width of about ten meters, and the multiple, parallel traces mean that the sonar beam was reflecting from several of the object's surfaces. The thin traces nearby are probably fish. (*Academy of Applied Science*)

The *Malaran*, the 33-foot cruiser used for sonar search for bones.
(*Klein Associates, Inc. and Academy of Applied Science*)

Martin Klein watches a sonar trace of the bottom of Loch Ness
emerge from the recorder. (*Jeffrey Thomason*)

A sonar trace of "Kleinhenge I," the mysterious, ancient stone circles found in Loch Ness. The multiple complex of interlocked circles is about 200 feet long. (*Klein Associates, Inc., and Academy of Applied Science*)

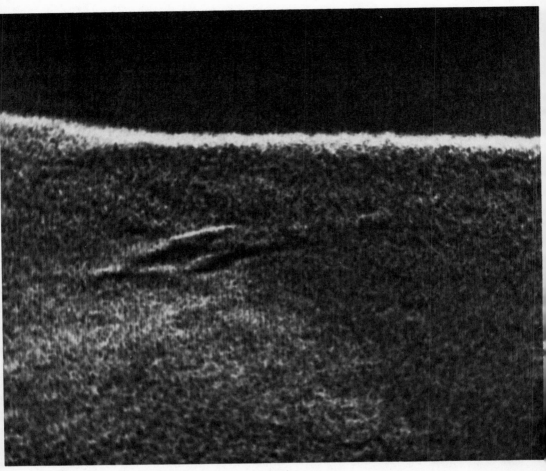

Sonar "picture" of the large, unknown object nicknamed "The Average Plesiosaur" found in the 1976 sonar search of the bottom. The object is about 30 feet long, and rests on the bottom of the loch in about 300 feet of water. (*Klein Associates, Inc., and Academy of Applied Science*)

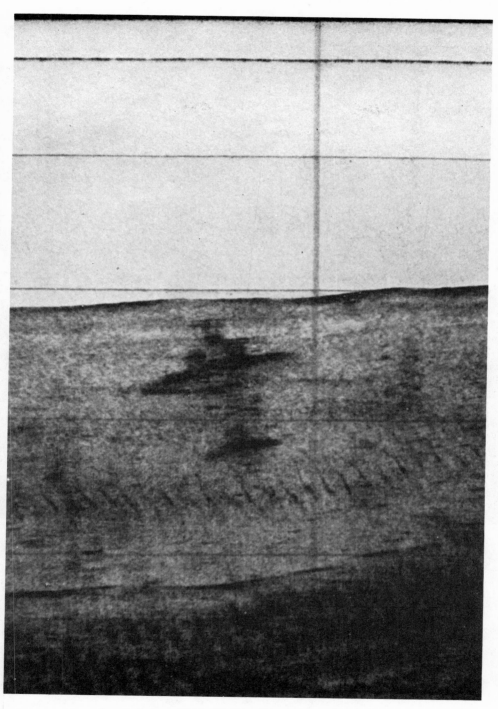

Sonar trace of World War II airplane discovered in the loch by the sonar team. (*Klein Associates, Inc., and Academy of Applied Science*)

The elasmosaur, a 40-foot prehistoric marine reptile is one candidate for the Loch Ness monster. (*Robert Ullrich*)

Underwater photo of a small section of the stone rings discovered in Loch Ness. (*Klein Associates, Inc., and Academy of Applied Science*)

 References

CHAPTER ONE

Meredith, Dennis L. "The Loch Ness Press Mess." *Technology Review*, March/April 1976, pp. 10–12.

Rines, Robert H., Edgerton, Harold E., Wyckoff, Charles W. and Klein, Martin. "Search for the Loch Ness Monster." *Technology Review*, March/April 1976, pp. 25–40.

"Nessie—At Last, the Full Fantastic Truth." *Sunday Mail*, Glasgow, Scotland, 23 November 1975.

Todd, Roger. "Nessie Is a Lump of Wood." *Daily Record*, Scotland, 25 November 1975.

Witchell, Nicholas. *The Loch Ness Story*. Baltimore: Penquin Books, 1975.

CHAPTER TWO

Scott, Peter and Rines, Robert. "Naming the Loch Ness Monster." *Nature*, 11 December 1975, pp. 466–68.

CHAPTER THREE

Dinsdale, Tim. *Loch Ness Monster*. London: Routledge & Kegan Paul, 1976.

Dinsdale, Tim. *Project Water Horse*. London: Routledge & Kegan Paul, 1975.

Douglas, John. "The Case for the Loch Ness Monster." *Science News*, 17 April 1976: 47–48.

Klein, Martin, Rines, Robert H., Dinsdale, Tim and Foster, Laurence S. "Underwater Search at Loch Ness." Boston, Mass.: Academy of Applied Science Monograph, 1972.

"*Nessiteras skeptyx.*" *Nature*, 25 December 1975, p. 655.
Sullivan, Walter, "Loch Ness Monster: A Serious View." *The New York Times*, 8 April 1976.
"Myth or Monster?" *Time*, 20 November 1972: 66.
"Nessie's Return." *Time*, 12 January 1976: 39–40.

CHAPTER FIVE

Costello, Peter. *In Search of Lake Monsters.* New York: Berkeley Publishing Corp., 1975.
Dinsdale. *Loch Ness Monster.*
Holgate, Norman. "Paleozoic and Tertiary Transcurrent Movements on the Great Glen Fault." *Scottish Journal of Geology* Vol. 5, No. 2 (1969), 97–139.
Inverness Field Club. *The Hub of the Highlands.* Edited by Paul Harris. Edinburgh: The Albyn Press, 1975.
Mackay, William. *Urquhart and Glenmoriston.* 1914.
MacLean, Calum I. *The Highlands.* Inverness: Club Leabhar Ltd., 1975.
Sossons, J. B., "The Quaternary in Scotland: A Review." *Scottish Journal of Geology*, Vol. 10, No. 4 (1974), 311–37.
Sullivan, Walter. *Continents in Motion.* New York: McGraw-Hill, 1974.
Witchell. *The Loch Ness Story.*

CHAPTER SIX

Dinsdale. *Loch Ness Monster.*
Gould, Rupert T. *The Loch Ness Monster and Others.* New York: University Books, 1969.
Holiday, F. W. *The Great Orm of Loch Ness.* London: Faber and Faber, 1968.
Hopson, Janet. "Fins to Feet to Fanclubs: An (Old) Fish Story." *Science News*, 10 January 1976: 28–30.
Mackal, Roy P. *The Monsters of Loch Ness.* Chicago: Swallow Press, 1976.
"Boat Was 'Surrounded by Monsters'." *Scotsman*, 14 July 1976.
Searle, Frank. "Monster in the Sky." *Daily Record*, 2 December 1974.
Whyte, Constance. *More Than a Legend.* London: Hamish Hamilton, 1957.
Wilkins, Alan. "Monster: The Four Vital Sightings." *The Field*, 27 November 1975, pp. 1047–48.
Wilkins, Alan. "The Shapes on the Loch." *The Field*, 4 December 1976.
Witchell. *The Loch Ness Story.*

CHAPTER EIGHT

Burl, Aubrey. *The Stone Circles of the British Isles.* New Haven: Yale University Press, 1976.

Klein, Martin and Edgerton, Harold. "Sonar—A Modern Technique for Ocean Exploration." *IEEE Spectrum*, June 1968, pp. 40–46.

Klein, Martin and Finkelstein, Charles. "Sonar Serendipity in Loch Ness." *Technology Review,* December 1976, pp. 44–57.

Klein, Martin. "Side-Scan Sonar." *Undersea Technology*, April 1967.

CHAPTER TEN

Blundy, David. "Nessie, This Is Your Best Show Yet." *London Sunday Times*, 30 November 1975.

Mackal. *The Monsters of Loch Ness.*

"Nessie: What's in an Anagram?" *Science*, 9 January 1976.

Pollak, Richard, "Monster Amok in Newsroom," *MORE*, July/August, 1976, pp. 57–58.

Swan, Jon. "Monster Swamps 'Times.'" *Columbia Journalism Review*, September/October 1976, pp. 42–44.